Contents

Spring

Summer

Foreword

The first thing I do when perusing a new book is to read the table of contents. If the chapter titles are cute or impossibly vague, I usually lay the book down. Who is willing to risk precious time in a chapter that promises nothing specific?

With few exceptions, the forty chapter titles in this book tell the reader what to expect. They are deliciously explicit. Take the first chapter: "Responsibilities Toward Outsiders." A typical Christian reader not only knows what to expect, he *wants* the promised information. Why he wants it is clear: each chapter deals with questions important to us as Christians. Who is not troubled at times by nagging doubt or a tendency to complain? This is an uncommonly practical book.

If the practical nature of *Thoughts for Growing Christians* first catches the eye, it's the book's second distinctive that makes it truly useful, which is the book's constant appeal to Scripture. *Thoughts for Growing Christians* is not "pop psychology" adapted to Christians; it is exposition and application of the Word of God. The first word in the text is from Colossians. What follows is a sane and attractive handling of two verses in that lovely epistle.

The book ends with a treatment of part of the Sermon on the Mount. Thus, it's filled with Scripture, from beginning to end.

A word in the title may be misleading. No one should make the mistake of thinking that "growing" restricts the book to young people. True, the author writes with students in mind, but all of us can learn a great deal from this book. This isn't watered-down material. This isn't the shallow stuff writers sometimes try to fob off on young people, as if young people were not yet discriminating enough to know triteness from truth. This is solid food, guaranteed to enrich the minds and souls of sincere seekers.

C. DONALD COLE
Radio Pastor
Moody Bible Institute

FALL

1

Responsibilities Toward Outsiders

Colossians 4:5-6 Conduct yourselves with wisdom toward outsiders, making the most of the opportunity. Let your speech always be with grace, seasoned, as it were, with salt, so that you may know how you should respond to each person.
Read Colossians 4:2-6.

The end of summer always brings with it the renewed responsibilities of the fall season. Requirements of studies and schedules can be heavy and can sometimes overwhelm us. But let us be careful that we don't get so busy that our responsibilities to outsiders are neglected. God informs us in Colossians 4:5-6 that we, as growing Christians, have certain constant duties toward outsiders.

Who are those outsiders, anyway? Does that word refer to people who are outside our denomination or church or circle of fellowship? No. The outsiders mentioned are non-Christians—those who are outside the family of God. Until a person acknowledges the Lord Jesus Christ as his own personal Savior, Scripture refers to him as an outsider. In Mark 4:11, Jesus referred to those who *only listened* to Him as outsiders. He proclaimed the good news to them and ministered to their needs, but until they believed in Him they were considered outsiders.

Several responsibilities toward outsiders are given to us in Colossians 4:5-6. First of all we are to conduct ourselves with wisdom toward outsiders. That has to do with our way of life and life-style. We have a responsibility to make sure that our walk in life is in line with Scripture. Outsiders are observing us. We are on display! Our actions must be consistent with what we preach. How consistent are we, for example, if we ride around with a bumper sticker that says, "Jesus is the Way," but then break the speed limit or cut in front of another driver? How consistent are we if we walk around with a New Testament in our pocket or purse, but then rip off ("borrow") paper from the office or tools from the shop or books from the library? How consistent are we if we are involved in a Christian outreach ministry on campus or in the community, but then show a bad attitude in front of the very people we are trying to reach? We must be extremely careful of how we're impressing outsiders, for at the slightest inconsistency unbelievers are quick to respond, "Your actions speak so loudly that I can't hear what you're saying!"

Yes, it is hard at times to be concerned about what others are thinking of our actions, but it's a responsibility God has given us. In 2 Corinthians 6:3 we are told to "give no cause for offense in anything, so that the ministry is not discredited." What a responsibility! In some situations with outsiders, it's hard to know exactly what course of action is not consistent with Scripture. Not every situation is as clear-cut as the examples given above. Do we demand that the non-Christian student who lives in the next room turn down his stereo while we're studying, do we suggest it, do we put up with the noise, or do we study elsewhere? Do we tell our non-Christian neighbor to do something about the dandelions in his lawn, which are spreading into our yard, or do we keep on buying weed killer, or do we let the dandelions spread and admire their beauty, or do we weed and feed his lawn too? Or should our priorities have anything to do with dandelions? Those *can* be difficult questions in certain situations. That is why our verse says that *wisdom* is called for in our conduct with outsiders. The promise of wisdom from above (James 1:5) certainly applies to us in such situations. God promises to give us that insight if we ask Him, so we really have no excuse for not conducting ourselves with wisdom toward outsiders.

Wise conduct can actually draw outsiders to Christ. In 1 Corinthians 10:31-33 we see that the apostle Paul was concerned about actions that would offend not only believers (the church of God), but outsiders as well (Jews or Greeks). He indicates that his wise conduct, even in eating and drinking (v. 31), could actually lead unbelievers to salvation (v. 33). Is our conduct available as a magnet for God to use in His concern for outsiders? Our way of life is the only Bible some unbelievers read.

A second responsibility that growing Christians have toward outsiders is to make the most of the opportunity. That does not mean to take advantage of unbelievers! The idea here is that we should look for the special opportunities in which we can communicate Christ to non-Christians. Situations will present themselves in which it is quite obvious that God has given us an opportunity to speak for Him. It may be in a classroom before other students where the question of God has been raised. It may be in a one-on-one discussion with some unbeliever concerning a contemporary issue like gay rights. It may be in small talk with a total stranger on a plane or bus. Those opportunities pop up all the time. The point of the Colossians passage is that we have a responsibility to take advantage of those special times when they come along. We are not to "blow it" by losing the opportunity.

Opportunities cannot be recaptured once they are missed.

Prayer concerning those special times is certainly an essential prerequisite for "making the most of the opportunity." Notice how the apostle Paul placed a great emphasis on prayer in the verses immediately preceding our text (4:2-4). He not only prayed that the doors would be opened for the Word but that he would be enabled to communicate the Word clearly. We too should pray for opportunities and for clarity of communication when God opens the door. "Lord, give me an opportunity to speak to my boss about You. May I speak in words he can understand." "Lord, help me to make the most of the opportunity when that questioning student comes to talk to me this afternoon about my faith. Guide me in the conversation and direct me in the selection of literature I should give to her." "Lord, You know how my non-Christian friend is going through hard times right now. May I not miss the opportunity to steer our talk and thoughts in Your direction." "Lord, help me to make the most of the opportunities that You will bring to me on my trip this weekend. Give me the guts to speak out for You—even to total strangers. Help me not to miss that once-in-a-lifetime opportunity to speak to that special individual that You're going to bring to my attention." All those prayers have a way of being answered more directly than we ever thought possible! Try it!

In verse 6 we are given a third responsibility toward outsiders. It specifically concerns our talk. Three characteristics of responsible talk are given here. Our talk should be gracious. Our talk should be salty. And our talk should be perceptive. Gracious talk is talk that is courteous, cordial, cheerful, controlled, compassionate, and Christlike. Gracious talk is free from bitterness and bad-mouthing. Needling a person we work with is not gracious talk. Sour grapes about our grades or our "sitting-on-the-bench" position on the team is not gracious talk.

Asking the slow driver in front of us if he bought his license at K-Mart is not gracious talk!

Although our talk with outsiders is to be gracious, it is not to be bland or compromising—it is to be salty. In the days before refrigeration, salt was used as a preservative. Meat was impregnated with salt to prevent the spread of decay and corruption. In the same way, our talk with unbelievers should have the effect of preventing the spread of spiritual and moral decay in this world. That is what the Lord Jesus meant when He said in Matthew 5:13 that we are the salt of this earth. We are not to be complacent in the midst of corruption. We should speak out against abortion and godless evolution. We should speak out against social injustice in the community, in the nation, and in the world. In our conversations with non-Christians, we have a responsibility to communicate the biblical system of values and standards.

Finally, our talk with outsiders should be perceptive. We not only have a responsibility to respond to unbelievers (as the end of verse 6 indicates); we have a responsibility to know *how* to respond to each unbeliever. Not every non-Christian is the same. We should not have a "canned" approach to outsiders. Our Lord approached different unbelievers in different ways depending on "where they were coming from." (Compare Matthew 23:27, 33; Mark 10:21; and John 4:16-18, for example.) Some outsiders need to hear about the love of God. Some outsiders need to hear about the judgment of God. Some outsiders need to have their legitimate questions about the faith answered (see 1 Peter 3:15). Some outsiders need to be challenged. We have a responsibility to be perceptive and sensitive to those different needs of unbelievers so that we "may know how to respond to each person." Praise God, we have the Holy Spirit to enable us to fulfill all those responsibilities to outsiders.

2

Unannounced Tests

Judges 7:4 Then the LORD said to Gideon, "The people are still too many; bring them down to the water and I will test them for you there."
Read all of Judges 6 and 7.

It's hard to believe, but it won't be long before midterm exams are upon us! That is not a very pleasant thought, but then again, taking exams isn't all that bad. Sure, there's always the pressure and the fear of failing, but at least you can prepare yourself mentally and emotionally for an exam. What really hurts are those unannounced tests that some teachers spring on you! Those pop quizzes can be devastating. From the teacher's perspective, however, unannounced tests are very revealing. They certainly separate the dedicated students from the last-minute crammers! And they invariably point out the difference in attitudes that students have toward their teachers as well as their studies.

God gives unannounced tests. Every growing Christian is a student in the school of God, and the Teacher has the policy of giving unannounced tests to measure our faith. Sometimes they are small quizzes; other times they are biggies. They can be administered anywhere and in any of our everyday life situations. These tests are so unannounced that many times we don't even know that we're being tested. But God knows, and He's watching to see how we do. He's interested in our whole approach to "studies" in His school, as well as our attitudes toward Him.

In Judges 7 we have the account of some unannounced tests that God gave some of His people during the days of Gideon. Judges ruled in Israel before the time of the kings, and Gideon was one of the judges who was used by God to deliver Israel from the Midianites. The Midianites were one of Israel's enemies who lived on the east side of the Jordan River. They had a unique way of keeping Israel in subjection. Every year the hordes of camel-riding Midianites would swarm across the Jordan into Israel's territory around harvest time. They would ravage the land, taking whatever crops they wanted and destroying the rest. They also took every sheep, ox, and donkey they laid their eyes on. That had gone on for seven straight years. No wonder many Israelites hid in mountain dens and caves as the Midianites approached, and no wonder they finally cried to the Lord. (See the background in Judges 6:1-6.) You see, the Lord had permitted Israel's defeat by the Midianites because of Israel's sin. Finally, after seven years of discipline, Israel got the message and turned again to the Lord. God's discipline for His people today, as well as in Gideon's day, is always programmed to turn wayward hearts back to Him (see Hebrews 12:3-11).

The first unannounced test that God gave His people could be called the "Who Will Answer?" test. The Midianites had swept across the Jordan for the eighth straight year of harvest looting (Judges 6:33). In the power of the Spirit of the Lord, Gideon sent out a call to the people to come and fight the enemy. That summons was the call of God. The appeal went out first to Gideon's own family, the Abiezrites; then to his own tribe in Israel, Manasseh; then finally to the surrounding tribes of Asher, Zebulun, and Naphtali (6:34-35). Many responded to the call—but not everyone. There were certainly more people in the combined tribes of Manasseh, Asher, Zebulun, and Naphtali than the 32,000 (7:3) that responded to God's call. Oh, there were probably many "good reasons" as well as obvious excuses for refusing the call. "A hopeless cause!" "Why should I submit to Gideon?" "Let the other tribes carry their fair share of the load!" "I'm too busy reinforcing my hideout in the mountains!"

The "Who Will Answer?" test is still being given to God's people today. The enemy of our souls is "ravaging the land" all around us. Satan is at work at your school and at your job. Moral standards and truth are up for grabs. God's call goes out to every growing Christian to join in the battle. The call is not just for foreign missionaries or those in the ministry, but for all of us. What are we doing to fight the enemy right where we are? Are we helping out with the thrust of Christian witness on campus, or are we running to the hideouts of delay and indecision? If we refuse to respond to the call, not only will the enemy continue his devastating work, but we will fail God's unannounced test.

A second unannounced test was given to Gideon and his followers in Judges 7:1-3. Let's call this test the "Who Is Afraid?" test. It was given when Gideon brought his recruits to the valley of Jezreel, where the enemy armies were camped. From the hills bordering the southern edge of that large valley, the Midianite camp could be seen stretched out below them. There were so many enemy troops that they looked like locusts covering the land—as numerous as the sand on the seashore (7:12)! Imagine yourself as one of the Israelite enlistees, getting your first glimpse of the enemy. "What am I getting myself into? I never realized what I was being called to do! I'm all for coming out of the caves, but not now. I'm going AWOL the first chance I get." Well, Gideon's men didn't have to wait very long before they got the chance to drop out and run home. The Lord said that anyone who was afraid could bail out immediately, and more than two-thirds of Gideon's army took the Lord at His Word! Little did they realize that they had just failed an unannounced test.

The Lord still administers the "Who Is Afraid?" test as a measure of our faith. He never forces us to fight if we want to run back to the shelter of our mountain hide-aways. But He does test us. Are we willing to stand up for the Lord when confronted by the enemy? Do we stand up (maybe *alone*) for the truth of the Bible in our English and Biology classes—even if it means a lower grade? Do we stand up for the absolute moral values of Scripture in the dorm or on the job—even though everyone else is apathetic? That not only takes courage, but a tested faith behind the courage.

In verses 4-7 of Judges 7, we see a third unannounced test that God gave to Gideon's followers. The "Who Is Alert?" test was given to the 10,000 brave soldiers who still hung in there after the first two quizzes. The third test was administered at the spring of water where they camped. Gideon's men never dreamed that they were being tested by the way they got a drink of water. But the way they quenched their thirst was very significant. It indicated whether they were alert to the enemy. If they carelessly got down on all fours to immerse their heads and mouths in the cool water, it was pretty obvious that they were more concerned about meeting their own needs than about getting on with the battle. If, on the other hand, they took the water up in their cupped hands and lapped it so they could still keep an eye out for the enemy, then it proved that they were alert and ready to move out for the battle. Only 300 men passed this test—only 3 percent!

Only a small percentage of Christians pass the "Who Is Alert?" test today. Faced with the enemy, we're more concerned about ourselves and our needs than with fighting the battles of the Lord. Ephesians 6:10-19 warns us that we are in a spiritual battle, and we dare not fail to be alert. We are not alert if we are more concerned about our physical comfort than about our spiritual condition. We are not alert if we are more concerned about our advances in this world than about enemy advances in our family or fellowship. Good intentions have never yet won a battle— or passed an unannounced test! As in Gideon's day, the *way* we go about meeting our basic needs is a good indication of "where we're at" spiritually, and whether we're passing the "Who Is Alert?" test.

Gideon's 300 men, who passed all three tests, were a pitifully small army—much less than 1 percent of the enemy's 135,000 men (Judges 8:10). We can imagine Gideon's shock (and faith!) as God whittled his army down to a mere handful. Gideon probably breathed a sigh of relief when God finally stopped saying, "You have too many people!" But how could a band of 300 men with trumpets and torches defeat 135,000 well-equipped men? No problem! One plus God is always a majority! Read the rest of Judges 7 and see how the Lord pulled off the victory with the 300 men whose faith was tested. That is always God's way. His choice soldiers are the students whose faith has been demonstrated by unannounced tests!

3

The Last Word

2 Timothy 3:16-17   All Scripture is inspired by God and profitable for teaching, for reproof, for correction, for training in righteousness; that the man of God may be adequate, equipped for every good work.

The beginning of a new school year can bring with it many unique challenges. One of your most vulnerable areas will be your Christian faith. For many in secular schools, the trauma will begin with a course in philosophy or religion (of all things!). The Bible will undoubtedly be mentioned again and again in your courses and discussions. You may hear so many "new things" about the Bible that you'll feel like you've been in a sheltered vacuum all your life. You may have so many new questions about the Bible that you'll be frustrated and confused and not know where to begin. But when all is said and done, the issue will come down to this very basic question: What is the Bible? It sounds pretty elementary, I agree, but think over the profound implications of that question before reading on.

Is the Bible merely a collection of man's highest and noblest thoughts about God down through history? Is the Bible simply the result of man's unending search for the divine? Is the Bible only a record of the various experiences of man worth passing on for the benefit and preservation of human society? Is the Bible just a "good book" containing what man has found to be timeless truth and the best moral values to live by? Is the Bible but a product of man's thinking relative to his constantly changing culture and therefore containing no absolute standards whatsoever? OR—Is the Bible what it claims to be: the Word of God?

The basic issue, then, is whether the Bible is man's words about God or God's Word to man. If the Bible is only man's words about God (great and beautiful though they may be), then some of its statements may be true but others may be slightly erroneous; it has no real basis for authority over my life. I may appreciate its insights. I may deem it worthy of study. I may respect its values. I may even follow its principles. But it does not have authority over me. No way! How can the accumulated wisdom of fellow creatures possibly make claims on *my* life and destiny? *I* am the master of my own ship. *I* have the last word on my own life!

But if the Bible is *God's* words to man, it is an entirely different story. If the Bible is God's words to man, then man cannot arbitrarily decide what in the Bible is true and what is a human error or miscalculation. God is not the author of lies or deceit or confusion. If the Bible is God's words to man, then man cannot pick and choose what values and standards in the Bible are applicable for today and what can be tossed aside as "cultural hang-ons." God does not lower or change His standards to adapt to society's whims. And finally, if the Bible is indeed God's words to man, as it claims, then it does have a basis for authority over my life. God is my Creator; He has spoken, and *He* is the last word.

Does the Bible really claim to be God's words to man? Yes, it certainly does! The Bible is full of statements such as, "Thus saith the Lord," and "This is the word of the Lord." The whole sense of Scripture is that God is speaking *to* man—not man speaking *about* God. The Old Testament prophets and the New Testament apostles were quite convinced that they were not just writing words about God but that they were communicating God's words to man in writing. The Bible's consistent claim to be the words of God to man is focused in 2 Timothy 3:16-17.

"All Scripture is inspired by God" has also been translated "All Scripture is given by inspiration of God" (KJV)* or "All Scripture is God-breathed" (NIV).† The term "God-breathed" gives us the correct idea of what inspiration is all about. Inspiration does not mean that man breathed out words about God, but that God breathed out words to man. In other words, the origin of Scripture is not the mind of man but the "mouth" of God. That is what our Lord had in mind when He said, "It is written: MAN SHALL NOT LIVE BY BREAD ALONE, BUT BY EVERY WORD THAT COMES FROM THE MOUTH OF GOD" (Matthew 4:4). The Lord Jesus considered the written Scriptures to be absolute authority because they were God-breathed. Notice how Jesus equates the writings of Moses with the words of God in Mark 7:9-13. Should we have a lower view of Scripture than our Lord had?

The Bible, then, is not inspired because man wrote about God during "moments of inspiration" as in the case of a poet, musician, or artist. And the Bible is not inspired because it stimulates or "inspires" men as in the case of a beautiful sunset or view from a mountain peak. No! The Bible is inspired because it is the "God-breathed" Word of God to man.

But the Bible sounds so human! Of course! God chose human languages and human thought patterns in order to communicate with humans. How else could He have done it? But doesn't that make the men who actually

*King James Version.
†*New International Version.*

penned the words mechanical robots who received dicta-
tion? Not at all! God used the human authors' own
personalities and writing styles as a channel of communication. But as sovereign God and Lord of all, He certainly
controlled and guarded and superintended the words that
went down on the parchments. Therefore the Bible is not
contaminated with errors—not even in the areas of historical and numerical data. What a difference between the
Bible and other writings of the same period! A brief
examination reveals how much the grotesque, the mythological, and the absurd is contained in those other
writings.

"OK," someone says, "so the Bible claims to be the
Word of God and seems to present some pretty good
credentials, but who's to say whether it really is or not?
I'm not going to submit to it until I can find a person
who is a real authority on the Bible and take *his* advice."
Sorry! The highest authority always has the last word. To
be consistent, we must let the Bible speak for itself—not
ask modern man (brilliant though he may be) to make
the final decision on the Bible.

Because the Bible *is* God's Word to man, matters of
doctrine and ethics are not up for grabs. It is not just one
man's words against another's. *God* has given us His
mind on those matters. We can come to the Bible and
read it as if God were speaking directly to us and we were
hearing the words right from His own mouth. That is
true of *all* of the Bible (2 Timothy 3:16). It is true that
correct interpretation comes into play here, and that is
another important matter. But receiving the Bible as
God's words to man is the first step. Now the Bible becomes
authoritative in our lives. We submit to it. We obey it. We
come to depend on the words of God in all important
matters (vv. 16-17). We come to know that the Bible has
the last word.

4

Discipline is Demanded

1 Corinthians 9:24-27   Do you not know that those who run in a race all run, but only one receives the prize? Run in such a way that you may win. And everyone who competes in the games exercises self-control in all things. They then do it to receive a perishable wreath, but we an imperishable. Therefore I run in such a way, as not without aim; I box in such a way, as not beating the air; but I buffet my body and make it my slave, lest possibly after I have preached to others, I myself should be disqualified.

2 Timothy 2:15   Be diligent to present yourself approved to God as a workman who does not need to be ashamed, handling accurately the word of truth.

2 Timothy 2:5   And also if anyone competes as an athlete, he does not win the prize unless he competes according to the rules.

The first few days back at school are the greatest, aren't they? There's plenty to talk about with old friends. Classes are not routine or boring yet (maybe because teachers come prepared for the first few days!). Assignment due dates still seem far away. At first everything is

27

exciting and "easy"—but soon the truth strikes! It's going to be another year of hard work and sweat! And without some kind of *discipline* in your life, you're not going to do well at all.

The point of the above Scripture is that discipline is also demanded in your life as a Christian. Some Christians have the idea that the *"Christian* life" should be like a summer vacation filled with surf, sun, and sleep. No way! The life of a growing Christian is more like the life of a good student or a good athlete—disciplined!

Think of the discipline demanded in the life of an athlete. His success doesn't begin at the time of the game or meet. First, he has a long, hard, disciplined training period. If you don't think that is true, go over and visit football practice some afternoon. You won't believe the grunts and groans you'll hear! You'll see guys so exhausted they can hardly stand—but still forcing themselves to put out and *run*.

The Greek games, which are the source of Paul's analogy in 1 Corinthians 9, included footracing, wrestling, and boxing, among other things. Verse 24 does not mean that only one person can win the prize in the "Christian race" but that all Christians should run as winners run. That is, we must be disciplined in training and in competing, as is every winning athlete. In the days of the Greek games there was the discipline of "self-control in all things" (1 Corinthians 9:25), such as strict diet, strenuous exercise, chastity, and curfew. Every aspect of the athlete's life was under discipline.

The application to the maturing Christian is obvious. We *must* exercise self-control when it comes to fun and sports and other wholesome activities. It's easy to become so busy doing good things that we have no evening left each week to meet with other Christians for fellowship and prayer. We *must* practice self-denial in things like excess sleep, TV, and magazine time to make room for prayer time. Verse 27 doesn't mean that you should beat your body with a baseball bat, but it *can* mean that you should set your alarm for 5:30 A.M. for time alone with the Lord. We must regulate our study time to include time for study of the Scriptures. We are commanded in 2 Timothy 2:15 to be diligent in this matter. If we are just reading a psalm for the day, then we are disobeying the Lord's command. "Handling accurately the word of truth" demands discipline. Approval by God is a lot different from mere approval by men. So let's get organized and begin to *study* a book in God's holy Word. We must purpose to make every action count. Otherwise, we are like blindfolded runners or shadowboxers. What a waste of time and energy!

Although the disciplined life is hard (even a drag at times), we are assured of reward that will last forever (1 Corinthians 9:25). If the runners in the Greek games so disciplined their lives for a mere wreath or garland of dead leaves, how much more should we discipline our lives when eternal values are at stake! 2 Timothy 2:5 reminds us that there is no wreath for one who breaks the rules of training or the rules of the race. Discipline must be maintained all the way through. Can you imagine a runner who is behind in the last lap cutting across the infield to catch up? Forget it! There is no short-cut to spiritual maturity either! We must be disciplined in keeping the rules for Christian growth that God has laid down in His Word. No discipline, no wreath!

5

Salt in Season

Matthew 5:13 You are the salt of the earth; but if the salt has become tasteless, how will it be made salty again? It is good for nothing anymore, except to be thrown out and trampled under foot by men.

Colossians 4:6 Let your speech always be with grace, seasoned, as it were, with salt, so that you may know how you should respond to each person.

It's happened again! Summer has turned into fall, and it seems that everything and everybody has got into the act. A beach bum turned into a student. A backpack turned into a pair of shoulder pads. A swimsuit turned into a sweater. And the burning summer sun turned into the burning midnight oil. Here's a suggestion: Let your summer sugar turn into September salt!

Jesus said in Matthew 5:13, "You are the salt of the earth." What did He mean by that? Flavor-people? No! Small insignificant grains in a large world? No! In what way are we the salt of the earth? A little background in the use of salt at the time of Christ will help. Before the days of refrigeration, salt was used as a preservative. You couldn't buy your meat and store it indefinitely in a freezer. Your only chance for delaying the decay and corruption of your steaks was to cover them with salt.

As Christians, we are to hold in check the spread of sin in this world. Our lives are to have the effect of preventing the advance of corruption, even though spiritual and moral decay may surround us. Jesus says that our presence in the locker room or college dorm should to some degree stifle the spread of sinful ideas, stories, or actions. Are you a grain of salt in the particular segment of society in which God has placed you? The Bible says in Colossians 4:6 that our speech or conversation must not only be nice (gracious) but also guarded and pungently powerful (seasoned with salt). And sometimes it really takes courage!

Salt is not a preservative because it does something to "cure" decay, but because its very nature prevents the *spread* of corruption. Just so, as Christians we cannot "cure" this world of sin, but the influence of our Christian living can and must arrest moral decay that is present in the world. Are you a Christian? Then you are a grain of salt that God has specifically placed in your school or job or wherever you are. There may not be too many other active grains around, so do your thing!

The Lord Jesus said that salt could become tasteless or lose its tang. In those days, the "salt" in Israel was often the mixed saline and earthy deposits from the Dead Sea flats, from which the salt could dissolve out, leaving only a tasteless and useless residue. When salt lost its pungent power, it could no longer be used as a preservative. It wasn't good for anything and was thrown out on the ground and walked on. Instead of preventing the spread of decay and corruption in our immediate surroundings, we become part of the problem. No longer are we active servants in the kingdom of our Lord. We've fallen down on the job, and the enemy has "walked all over us!" Our lives and voices are now powerless and silent. (Read Revelation 3:15-16 for parallel thoughts.)

Every September on every campus the process of spiritual and moral decay begins its activity once again. Salt is needed! God may have given you a sweet sugar summer, but now He's looking for September salt. "You are the salt of the earth."

6

Controlled Circumstances

Philippians 1:12-14   Now I want you to know, brethren, that my circumstances have turned out for the greater progress of the gospel, so that my imprisonment in the cause of Christ has become well known throughout the whole praetorian guard and to everyone else, and that most of the brethren, trusting in the Lord because of my imprisonment, have far more courage to speak the word of God without fear.
Read Philippians 1:12-21.

Circumstances in the life of the growing Christian don't just happen. They are controlled! Humanly speaking, our circumstances may be a blast or a bummer; they may be pleasant or tragic; they may be just or unfair; they may change overnight or stay the same for years. Divinely speaking, our circumstances are controlled as to what, when, where, and why. From our point of view, our circumstances may appear at times to be completely out of control; from God's, our circumstances are *never* out of control. Romans 8:28 says that for those who love Him, "God causes all things to work together for good." That certainly means control of all circumstances in the lives of growing Christians.

"Hey, wait a minute," you say. "If God is in control, then what about all those circumstances affecting me that involve injustice and cruelty and suffering and other forms of evil? What kind of control is that? And what about my circumstances when I sin? If God is in control of the circumstances, has He programmed me into sin?"

Of course not! The Bible teaches that when we sin it is our own fault and we cannot pin the blame on God (see James 1:13-15). But even when we sin, it doesn't mean that God has lost control of the situation. He may use the very circumstances in which we failed to teach us a lesson and draw us back to Him. Furthermore, the Bible never teaches that all the circumstances surrounding a Christian are good. Romans 8:28 does not say that all things are good. It says God causes all things to *work together* for good in the life of a Christian. Many circumstances affecting the Christian are anything but good. Your circumstances right now may be very bad. In fact, the Bible teaches that circumstances touching a Christian can be quite evil—and even manipulated by Satan himself! Read Job 1:6—2:10. Notice two points from that passage in Job. First we see that although God *permitted* evil circumstances to strike Job, God was not the source of the evil. (See also James 1:16-17 in this connection.) Only good things come from God; we are deceived if we don't believe that. Second, we see that God never lost control of Job's circumstances, but rather used them (evil and all) for His own purposes. He caused them to "work together for good" in Job's life. Read the rest of Job and see how God used those circumstances as a test of Job's faith. So God *is* in control of all of our circumstances. Although we are free to commit sin, and in spite of Satan's power (limited power—it's like he's on a leash temporarily, awaiting final judgment), God is still in control of our circumstances. Things are never out of control!

If ever there was a time when circumstances seemed to be out of control, it was during the final week of the life of our Lord. Consider the unfair trial of the Man who was completely innocent. Think of the physical abuse of the One who had harmed no one. Remember the cruel and untimely death of the Person who was so involved in helping mankind. Out of control? No, *in* control from start to finish! Of all the Old Testament prophecies about the final week, not a single prediction was missed or incomplete! Out of those "tragic" circumstances God gave us the greatest demonstration of His love and secured our eternal salvation. Now if God so overruled and controlled those seemingly chaotic circumstances, we can be sure that circumstances in our lives are not out of control. We can *"know* that God causes all things to work together for good"* in the lives of growing Christians.

In Philippians 1:12-17 we have a striking example of how God caused some unfortunate circumstances in the life of the apostle Paul to work together for good. When Paul wrote Philippians, he was awaiting his trial before Caesar in Rome. The possibility of death by the Roman sword was a reality he had to face each day. Pretty heavy circumstances! Already Paul had spent about two years in prison in Palestine while the establishment played politics with his case. It seemed as if circumstances were out of control. Paul had appealed to Caesar, and so he was finally brought to Rome to wait for his case to come up before the highest court in the Empire. While Paul waited, he was put under house arrest. That meant he was not thrown into a dungeon but was kept under arrest in his own rented house (see Acts 28:30-31). However, it was still imprisonment (Philippians 1:13), because a Roman soldier was always there on guard. In fact, Paul and the guard were chained together at all times. Because the escape of a Roman prisoner would cost the life of the Roman guard, there was no bail system in those days.

The chain was always there! Now the chain was several feet in length and allowed the prisoner a little movement, but think of the inconvenience and annoyance. Every word that Paul spoke was monitored. Every curse and obscene remark of the Roman soldiers had to be tolerated by Paul. He could not walk away. He had no privacy for his personal needs. The chain was always there. How could God allow such circumstances? For the guards it was only so many hours of duty and then they were free, but for Paul it was the same hard circumstances day after day. What possible good could come out of that situation? Was God still in control?

There was one further circumstance in Paul's life at that time that was hard to handle—maybe the hardest of all. From Philippians 1:15-17 we learn that some other Christians in Rome who sometimes disagreed with Paul were taking advantage of the situation. Because of their jealousy of the apostle, they were bad-mouthing Paul and proclaiming the Christian message to gain a prominent position for themselves in the Christian fellowship. If ever there was a Christian who had a legitimate right to complain about his circumstances, it was Paul. Cut off from a very successful and fruitful ministry; shut up in a house and constantly watched; put down by the very brothers and sisters he was trying to serve. Can you identify with Paul a little at this point? Yet Paul never complained about his circumstances. In fact, he was able to rise above them and rejoice in them (see Philippians 2:17 and 4:12). Why? Because he knew that God was causing those circumstances to work together for good.

Paul elaborates on some of the good results of his circumstances in Philippians 1:12-14. First there was the greater progress of the gospel (v. 12). All the imperial guards had heard about Christ (v. 13). It was impossible to be chained to the apostle Paul and not hear the good news about Jesus! You can imagine how word of their unique prisoner and his cause quickly circulated within the ranks of the soldiers—and filtered out to everyone else (v. 13). Apparently anyone who was interested or curious was allowed to come and visit Paul (see Acts 28:30-31). Soon the good news was even being heard and believed by servants (and maybe officials) in Caesar's household (Philippians 4:22). God was using Paul's "regrettable circumstances" to penetrate barriers that, up till now, had seemed impossible. Think of it—the gospel spreading to the heart of the Roman Empire because Paul's rights and freedom had been taken away. God *was* in control of those contrary circumstances. Is it possible that God has permitted you to be placed in a dorm, class, job, neighborhood, relationship, or hospital bed that is not exactly to your liking? Maybe that is the way God has chosen to reach someone "special" with the love and good news of Jesus Christ. You've been chosen because no one else could handle the particular situation.

Philippians 1:14 tells us that another good result was the greater courage of most of the Christians to spread the Word of God. It took quite a lot of courage to preach Jesus Christ in pagan Rome. It was much easier to be a "secret Christian" than to risk your life for what you believed. But the Christians in Rome were "turned on" by Paul's circumstances. If Paul could take so much abuse for the cause of Christ, they could certainly take a little heat too! Even the Christians who were jealous of Paul were at least made bold enough to get out and proclaim Christ, and for that Paul rejoiced (1:18). Because Paul's freedom was restricted and his rights taken away, Christians were encouraged to carry on the work boldly. Is it possible that God has allowed some of your freedom to be restricted and some of your rights to be yanked away from you? Maybe because of the way you handle those limitations, other growing Christians will be encouraged to get excited and carry on the work of the Lord. God has chosen *you* to be the example, so *He* can multiply the good results.

God caused all kinds of good things to come out of Paul's unfavorable circumstances. During his imprisonment, Paul had more time to write, and four books of the Bible were written: Philippians, Ephesians, Colossians, and Philemon. In the same way, God is working all of our circumstances together in accordance with His good purposes. Don't be discouraged! The Lord is in complete control!

7

Dealing With Doubts

John 20:24-25 But Thomas, one of the twelve, called Didymus, was not with them when Jesus came. The other disciples therefore were saying to him, "We have seen the Lord!" But he said to them, "Unless I shall see in His hands the imprint of the nails, and put my finger into the place of the nails, and put my hand into His side, I will not believe."

Luke 7:20 And when the men had come to Him, they said, "John the Baptist has sent us to You, saying, 'Are you the Expected One, or do we look for someone else?'"

Matthew 14:29-30 And He said, "Come!" And Peter got out of the boat, and walked on the water and came toward Jesus. But seeing the wind, he became afraid, and beginning to sink, he cried out, saying, "Lord, save me!"

How do you deal with your doubts about the Christian faith? You say you don't have any? Never, ever? Well, it's great if you can say that, but most of us growing Christians must confess that a few doubts do harass us every

now and then. In fact, some Christians are so loaded
down with doubts that they hardly ever get a chance to
rejoice in their salvation. Is there any solution to the
problem of doubts in the life of a Christian? Yes! The
Bible is sufficient for all we need to know in order to live
a godly life (2 Timothy 3:16-17). The Bible gives the
answers for dealing with doubts.

Basically, the biblical solution to doubts is *more faith*.
Ephesians 6:16 says that the shield of faith will "extin-
guish all the flaming missiles of the evil one." Doubts are
one of those flaming missiles. They are a part of the
strategy of Satan to keep the Christian off balance and
afraid and discouraged. Increased faith is the key to
dealing with doubts—it is a protective shield that keeps
doubts from getting to us. More faith does not mean
trying to psych ourselves up, or kissing our brains good-
bye, or some other type of subjective mental gymnastics.
No, it means looking more to, trusting more in, and
depending more on the Lord Jesus Christ. A little child
on his first trip to the big city with his father may be
bombarded with doubts and fears—his safety, his security,
his insignificance. His doubts are not dispelled by some
kind of subjective thinking ("I have no doubts, I have no
doubts, I have no doubts"), but by placing his little hand
in the firm grip of his father's big hand.

The Scriptures above are taken from three accounts in
the gospels where the Lord Jesus deals with doubts in the
lives of His followers. Before proceeding further, it would
be helpful for you to read the whole of each account. For
the doubts of Thomas read John 20:19-29. For the experience of John the Baptist read Luke 7:18-23. And for the
case of Peter read Matthew 14:22-33. God has included
those accounts in His Holy Word so that growing Christians may learn the lessons of what to do about doubts. In
each case there is a principle given to us for dealing with
doubts. When those principles are applied, faith will

increase and doubts will decrease.

"Doubting Thomas" is an example of a Christian who has doubts because he doesn't have enough visible or tangible evidence of God. Expecting always to see and touch (John 20:25) is an unreasonable attitude for a Christian and does not bring the blessings of the Lord (v. 29). Notice the circumstances. Thomas was not with the other disciples when Jesus came (v. 24). We don't know whether it was because of fear, lack of interest, or "business," but there may be a lesson here for us. If we don't get together for fellowship and study and prayer with other Christians, it won't be long before doubts come our way. We are not immune from doubts concerning the very fundamentals of the faith—Thomas doubted the resurrection of Jesus Christ. Thomas had his doubts dispelled, but not before he was back where he belonged with the other Christians.

The principle for increasing faith and decreasing doubts that is given to us in this account is that we must stay in close fellowship with our brothers and sisters in the Lord. One of the great truths of the New Testament is embodied in our Lord's words in Matthew 18:20: "For where two or three have gathered together in My name, there I am in their midst." There is nothing that will dispel our doubts more quickly than the living presence of the Lord. Although Thomas had the unique privilege of physically seeing the resurrected Christ in their company (v. 26), the Lord assures us that that is unnecessary (v. 29). Jesus continues to dwell in the midst of His people by His Spirit today (Ephesians 2:22). No wonder we are told in Hebrews 10:25 not to give up meeting together. The Christian "hermit" is more prone toward doubt than the Christian who is enjoying the Lord's presence in the midst of His people.

In the case of John the Baptist we have an example of a Christian who has doubts because he can't quite figure out what God is doing. At that time John was in prison (Matthew 11:2), and he could not understand why Jesus—the Messiah whom he had announced—wasn't moving a little faster to set things straight. Why was evil Herod still on the throne and ungodly Rome still in control of the land of Israel? Why was John sitting around in prison where he couldn't be effective? No wonder he sent to Jesus to ask, "Are you the Expected One, or do we look for someone else?" Note that John was not denying the Lord or giving up the faith. He was questioning matters he couldn't understand. Remember that the word "doubt" does not necessarily imply *denial;* it can mean to question, or hold questionable. But intellectual questions can lead to an attitude that is not pleasing to God. It is not wrong to question things we don't fully understand (such as "Why does God permit suffering in the world?"), but those questions should be approached in such a way that they will not make us "stumble" in our relationship with the Lord (v. 23).

The Scriptural approach to the hard questions is to bring them before the Lord and ask Him. To speculate and philosophize apart from prayer is to *question* God rather than *ask* God, and that is the wrong approach. Praying is not a cop-out; it is an ackowledgment of our dependence on the One who has all the answers. John the Baptist had some hard questions, so he sent directly to the Lord and waited. The Lord answered John by pointing him to the Scriptures. You see, John the Baptist knew the Old Testament prophecies like the back of his hand. All Jesus did was to show John that the prophecies of Isaiah concerning the coming Messiah were being fulfilled (see Isaiah 35:5-6). John was not delivered from prison—he was beheaded there—but God's Word was sufficient to answer John's doubts. Often the Lord will use His Word to answer our intellectual doubts. Here then is another principle for dealing with doubts. Lay them out before the Lord in prayer and wait on Him for His answer from the Word.

In the case of Peter's walking on the water, we have an example of a Christian who has doubts because the situation seems too impossible, even for God. Throughout the whole account, we have a picture of the walk of faith to which our Lord calls us (Matthew 14:29), across the troubled and contrary "sea of life." Peter began to sink because he took his eyes off the Lord to look at the storm. At that point his faith ebbed, and he began to doubt (v. 30). Looking at the contrary winds and crises waves of this life will always bring discouragement and fear. The protective shield of faith is lowered, and doubts concerning the Lord's ability zero in. The only cure for such doubts is to get our eyes back on the Lord in complete dependence, as Peter was forced to do (v. 31).

The principle of dealing with doubts that comes to us from the account of Peter is not just "Keep your eyes on the Lord," but "Be in a position where you *must* keep your eyes on the Lord." You see, the other disciples were safe in the boat and not in a position to experience the removal of doubts in the same way as Peter. Although Peter experienced "sinking," he also experienced "walking on water." It is only as we take the risk of walking by faith rather than sight that doubts concerning the Lord's ability to handle impossible situations are removed. Have you ever been in a situation where you had to cry out, "Lord, save me!" (v. 30)? To see and experience the Lord's power in those situations is to have doubts removed. Maybe the Lord wants you to serve Him this summer as a missionary helper or camp counselor or evangelistic team member. Are you holding back because it means a lower salary (or no salary), or for some selfish reason? Are you prepared to release your hold on whatever "boat" you are clinging to? The outstretched hand of the living Lord is ready to take hold of you and increase your faith (v. 31).

We've seen from these Scriptures that doubts are not uncommon to the followers of the Lord Jesus. As growing Christians, let us not be surprised if occasionally we find ourselves in the company of Thomas and John the Baptist and Peter. However, the Lord does not exactly praise their position. In fact, in each case there is a mild rebuke directed at the doubter. (See Matthew 14:31, Luke 7:23, and John 20:29.) God does not want us to flounder in doubts; He expects us to deal with them according to the principles He has included in His Word.

8

Dare to Be a Daniel

Daniel 1:8 But Daniel made up his mind that he would not defile himself with the king's choice food or with the wine which he drank; so he sought permission from the commander of the officials that he might not defile himself.

Read the whole first chapter of Daniel.

The battle of Carchemish in 605 B.C. is well known to students of ancient history. Nebuchadnezzar of Babylon defeated Pharaoh Necho of Egypt and began to take more and more control of the Near East. It wasn't long before Nebuchadnezzar made his first attack against Jerusalem. Although the ancient city of Jerusalem was not destroyed by Nebuchadnezzar until approximately eighteen years later, it was the beginning of the end for the kingdom of Judah. Long gone were the days of glory under David and Solomon. Many of the Jewish prophets had warned the people with the message from God that sorrowful days would come if they would not get right with the Lord. But the people of God would not turn back from their idolatry and immorality; they continued in their evil ways. So the Lord sent His people into captivity that they might learn the hard way. Although God is patient and loving, He must always be true to His word!

With the initial attack Nebuchadnezzar carried off a portion of the treasures of the Temple and took some choice male captives with him to Babylon. By taking some of the nobility as hostages, Nebuchadnezzar could control the rest of the royal family who remained as puppet rulers in Jerusalem. Thus the kingdom of Judah, which could have had the continued blessing of God, came under the control of pagan Babylon (Daniel 1:1-3).

The story of Daniel takes place during those dark days of captivity. It comes as a welcome light in the darkness. It is the thrilling account of how a few faithful individuals were blessed and honored by God in the midst of a situation that appeared hopeless. The story of Daniel contains some powerful lessons for Christians today—especially for the growing Christian who is faced with the temptation to compromise in his faith.

Daniel was one of four college-age, or perhaps high school-age, captives who decided to remain faithful to God in that foreign situation, no matter what the cost. Those four guys were a minority group for sure! The rest of the captives apparently could not withstand the pressure and submitted to the commands of Nebuchadnezzar. The fact that the majority of the captives compromised in their faith and conformed to the way of Babylon is not altogether surprising. Many Christians do the same thing today when they find themselves in non-Christian environments. For example, a Christian teenager leaves his home situation where he was safe and secure in a beautiful circle of Christian friends and fellowship, and arrives in the "big city" or on the secular college campus. There will be a tendency for that Christian to hide or relax his faith. The temptation to compromise and conform is very great. Almost unconsciously he will begin to justify his compromise.

The majority of the captives probably reasoned that it

was foolish to put their lives on the line when they were so far away from home and up against such overwhelming odds. Why not lie low and conform to the Babylonian way of life? When in Babylon do as the Babylonians do! After all, Nebuchadnezzar had saved their lives and was even giving them a three-year scholarship to the University of Babylon (v. 5). He had handpicked them and was training them for future diplomatic service. When they graduated, they would be bilingual and bicultural and would probably be sent on foreign missions for the king—maybe even back to the homeland.

How exciting! Why ruin such a future by verbalizing their faith? Why risk their lives when a little compromise would eliminate so many problems and so much emotional stress? The least they could do would be to conform to the demands of the king and eat his choice food and drink. If they were silent now, maybe they could get a word in for God later—after they had established a reputation for being good students and decent people. A little compromise now might even be a "subtle" way of reaching the Babylonians when the time was right. Why force things and be so outspoken about their faith?

They may have felt that God didn't care anyway. After all, weren't they down here in Babylon because God had given up on them? Why try to make amends once you've blown it with God? Maybe the best thing to do now would be to "put it in neutral and coast." Maybe after graduation things would change and it would be easier and safer and more logical to go back to the "faith of the fathers." Yes, the majority reasoned that way—they usually do! With "common sense" they rationalized themselves right out of the will of God (Daniel 1:4-7).

"But Daniel made up his mind that he would not defile himself . . ." (v. 8). Daniel knew from the Word of God that to eat at the king's "training table" was wrong. Not only were certain of those foods expressly forbidden to the Jews by the Old Testament, but also the king's food was probably dedicated to heathen idols. Eating and drinking the king's choice food would have involved Daniel in pagan religious practices. Daniel would not compromise and disobey the Word of God. He knew that God does not "water down His Word" because of uncomfortable or tough or "sticky" situations. God is pleased when we dare to be Daniels.

Daniel boldly took his stand (vv. 9-16). He did not give up when it looked like his first approach had failed (v. 10). This was no "sign from heaven" that he could go ahead and compromise and join the crowd. The very fact that his request was shelved—but not denied—encouraged Daniel to try a different and more tactful approach (vv. 11-14). Daniel persevered in his determination to find a way to obey the Lord in a seemingly impossible situation, and the way was opened up (see Luke 11:9-10). We also see that God was working behind the scenes on behalf of those faithful individuals. "*God* granted Daniel favor . . ." (Daniel 1:9). "*God* gave them knowledge . . ." (v. 17). God is always working behind the scenes for those who are determined to be faithful to Him—even when it doesn't appear so on center stage.

Now it should be pointed out that Daniel's refusal to compromise or conform to the ways of Babylon did not mean that he divorced himself completely from the new culture into which God had brought him. He accepted the new Babylonian name that was given to him (v. 7). He changed his language and life-style somewhat. (He even wrote part of the book of Daniel in Aramaic, which was the Babylonian language.) He did not become a dropout at the University of Babylon, but studied hard, and with the Lord's help he graduated *summa cum laude* (vv. 17-20). But Daniel did not compromise in matters of the faith. Although he adjusted and accommodated himself to his new environment, he did not conform to

Babylon. Babylon's goals did not become Daniel's goals.
Babylon's glories did not become Daniel's glories. Babylon's gods did not become Daniel's gods. Daniel did not
disobey the Word of God, or compromise in his faith. He
did not conform to this world. Daniel dared to stand
faithful.

Daniel's stand was no doubt costly. Imagine the comments of the other captives—even old buddies from home.
"What's Daniel trying to prove anyhow?" "He's going to
get us all killed!" "Here comes Deacon Daniel!" "Quit
trying to play God, Daniel!" And imagine having to eat
vegetables and water for three years—not too exciting (v.
16)! No, it wasn't easy, but Daniel made up his mind that
he was going to be faithful to the Lord. He set the
example, and three others followed—only three! A pitiful
minority, but God blessed and honored those faithful
few. Read on in Daniel and see how God promoted those
men and used them for His glory. We learn from verse 21
that Daniel outlived the Babylonian empire itself. (Cyrus
was a king of the Persian empire.) Notice how the Scripture seems to emphasize that Daniel *continued*—he continued to stand faithful to the Lord.

Right now many of you are facing a situation similar
to Daniel's. You've just started college or moved to a new
town or started a new job. You're in a different environment—maybe even a different culture. Everything's
changed. No one seems to talk about the Lord. Christians
are definitely in the minority. Home is so far away. The
pressure to conform to the new group is so great. It is so
easy to compromise—even just a little—in the faith.
What should you do? Dare to be a Daniel! Yes, it will be
hard and costly and very lonely at times. You will be
laughed at by some, mocked by others, and ignored by
many. The temptation to quit or lie low or crawl into
your shell will be very strong. Don't yield. Struggle to be
faithful!

Of course there will be changes. Any new situation brings adjustments. Some of you are coming from sheltered environments. Your horizons will be broadened. Daniel's certainly were. Your life-style will change some. God expects you to relate to the culture in which He places you. But God expects you to remain faithful to Him—in your social life, in your sex life, in your spoken life. Don't disobey the Word of God. Don't conform to this world's goals and glories and gods (Romans 12:2). Don't compromise! Be faithful, and God will bless you and honor you and use you for His glory. Dare to be a Daniel!

9

Proclamation of Liberty

Luke 4:18-19 THE SPIRIT OF THE LORD IS UPON ME, BECAUSE HE ANOINTED ME TO PREACH THE GOSPEL TO THE POOR. HE HAS SENT ME TO PROCLAIM RELEASE TO THE CAPTIVES, AND RECOVERY OF SIGHT TO THE BLIND, TO SET FREE THOSE WHO ARE DOWNTRODDEN, TO PROCLAIM THE FAVORABLE YEAR OF THE LORD.
Read Luke 4:14-30.

Fourth of July celebrations call our attention to the principles on which this country was founded—political and religious freedom—"with liberty and justice for all." Election Day reminds us that we still have considerable civil liberty and power of choice—we do not live under a dictatorship or military regime.

Hey, wait a minute! Let's stop the flag-waving and nostalgia and take a harder look at actual conditions in our country. Isn't it a stretch of the imagination to say that there is liberty and justice for *all?* And look at our elections. Do we really have a choice? We must admit that the hard look at our country reveals much that we cannot "wave the flag" about.

The Lord Jesus Christ came into this world and proclaimed liberty. The liberty He proclaimed was not im-

mediate political and religious freedom. It was not instant
relief from financial burdens and other problems. The
liberty that Jesus proclaimed was far more important—
liberty for the individual souls of people. He proclaimed
freedom from sin—freedom from the power and control
of sin; freedom from the direct effects and eternal consequences of sin. The liberty that Jesus proclaimed, then,
was not quite the same as what we sing about in "My
country 'tis of thee, Sweet land of liberty."

Therefore the growing Christian is not exactly a "flag-
waver"! Yes, we are thankful to the Lord for whatever
political and religious freedom we have—and you'd better
believe we've got a lot compared to many of our brothers
and sisters throughout the world. Furthermore, in spite
of shortcomings and problems and evil that exist throughout the government, we are thankful for the liberty and
justice that are still present in this land. But as true
Christians who are members of the Body of Christ around
the world, we recognize that our main concern is not to
wave the American flag. It is, rather, to reach out to the
individual souls with whom we are in contact and to
proclaim the liberty that the Lord Jesus still offers.

In Luke 4 the Lord announced the liberty He came to
proclaim. It is early in our Lord's three years of ministry;
the scene is a synagogue in Nazareth, where Jesus spent
His boyhood. The fact that Jesus regularly attended the
synagogue (v. 16) should be a lesson to us. The Lord
certainly recognized that there were many hypocrites in
the synagogues who misused and misapplied and misunderstood the Word of God. The Lord certainly recognized that the synagogues were not the "ideal church."
(Synagogues weren't even instituted by God in the Old
Testament—they arose mainly during the four hundred
years between the Old Testament and the New Testament.)
The Lord certainly realized that it was only a matter of
time before His proclamation of liberty would completely

do away with the synagogue system. Yet in spite of all the hypocrisies and imperfections, the Lord regularly attended the synagogue. Why? Because the Word of God was at least read and revered there. Do you see a lot of imperfections in the church you're attending? Are you disillusioned with the hypocrisies of some of the people who attend there? Don't just quit going to church! If the Word of God is read and proclaimed there, stick with it! Let's not get hung up with the hypocrites in our churches and the problems and faults they may have. Rather, let us personally continue to do our part there, proclaiming the liberty of Jesus Christ.

In the synagogue services of those days, after the preliminaries of prayer and a reading from the Law, any male who was of age could stand up to read and teach the Scriptures. On this occasion, Jesus stood up and read from the book of Isaiah, which was handed to Him by the synagogue attendant. The Lord purposely unrolled the precious handwritten Hebrew scroll to the place where it was prophesied that the Messiah would proclaim liberty when He came (vv. 17-19). How did our Lord know where to look for those words in the large and cumbersome scroll? Jesus had studied and learned the Scriptures as He was growing up there in Nazareth. And it wasn't easy! He didn't have a pocket testament to read in study hall or before He went to bed at night. Before the invention of the printing press, handwritten copies of the Scriptures were hard to come by, and the sacred Scriptures were kept mainly in the synagogues. A constant and determined effort had to be made to get to the local synagogue and literally "burn the midnight oil." How often Jesus must have left the carpenter shop and gone straight to the synagogue to study the Scriptures until late at night. What a lesson for those of us who almost reluctantly spend a few minutes (if that) each day reading the Word of God—we who have the Bible readily available to us at arm's reach!

The Lord read to the people from Isaiah 61:1-2. Notice that the first person is used, and the whole object of the Messiah's mission is announced—to proclaim the liberty that only He can bring to mankind. It is very significant that the Lord left out the last part of Isaiah 61:2, which says, "to proclaim . . . the day of vengeance of our God." Why? Because the day of judgment had not arrived! It will come when Christ returns. Right now it is still the "favorable year of the Lord." The liberty from the shackles and oppression and blindness of sin which Christ offered (Luke 4:18-19) is still available. The good news that Jesus announced was authenticated by His physical miracles, such as the literal recovery of sight to the blind (v. 18). But the main emphasis of our Lord's announcement was that liberty from both the present control and the eternal consequences of sin was now available through Him.

Jesus finished reading the Scripture and then, according to the custom of teaching and preaching in the synagogue, He sat down to explain the passage He had just read. Everyone there knew that this Scripture was speaking of the Messiah who was to come some day, and they were eagerly waiting to hear what Jesus would say about it (v. 20). Think of the drama of the moment when Jesus said, "*Today* this Scripture has been fulfilled in your hearing" (v. 21). Never before had such words been spoken in Israel! At first the people were impressed with the words of Christ (v. 22), but only because they did not catch the full implication of His claim. The people of Nazareth had known Jesus as the good and honest young carpenter who was associated in the trade with His father, Joseph. Now, after spending some time in Judea (v. 14), their gifted carpenter was emerging before their very eyes as a gifted speaker! How wonderful! But the Lord Jesus knew the truth about them. They were ready to receive

Him as a great carpenter and speaker, but not as God—only Joseph's son (v. 22)! How true that is today. Many people accept Jesus as anything from "a man of peace" to Superstar—but not as God!

In verses 23-27 the Lord proceeded, step by step, to uncover the real heart of the people. He knew their attitude would soon change when they heard the *full* proclamation of liberty. They would want to see His miraculous works but not accept His mandatory words (vv. 23-24). The liberty that Jesus proclaimed would only come if there was repentance of pride, of unbelief, of sin. The Lord drove that point home with two illustrations from the Old Testament. Because of Israel's unrepentant attitude at the time of the prophets Elijah and Elisha, God purposely withheld His acts of mercy from the Jews and extended His blessing to individual non-Jews who believed in Him. The widow of Zarephath (1 Kings 17) and Naaman the Syrian (2 Kings 5) were Gentiles who had faith in the living God of Israel (Luke 4:25-27). In the same way, the unrepentant and unbelieving attitude of Israel at the time of Christ would result in the blessings of the proclamation of liberty being largely withheld from the Jewish nation, and going out instead to individuals of any nation who would repent and believe.

As the need for repentance and faith was made clear to the people, they reacted in anger (v. 28). The reaction today is the same! When the liberty that Christ offers is shown to include the necessity of repentance from sin, and faith in the Lord Jesus as *God*, people get uptight. No one gets mad when Jesus is proclaimed as a great man who did good things, but when He is proclaimed as God, before Whom we sinners must repent, the reaction is different. People get angry when the good news is fully proclaimed. All Christians have a responsibility to present the *full* message of the gospel. We compromise the truth if we just say that Jesus wants to be "your friend."

We stop short of the total proclamation of liberty if we do not stress the necessity of repentance from sin *and* submission to the Lord Jesus Christ. When people hear that side of the proclamation of liberty, many of them jump off the "Jesus bandwagon"—even in anger!

The synagogue service broke up irreverently, as the people tried to do away with Jesus violently (v. 29). The religious false front of the people was gone. Jesus had exposed their real hearts of unbelief. But they could not do away with Christ—He simply walked *away* from them (v. 30). Jesus was always within easy reach of those who wanted to receive Him, but out of reach of those who rejected Him. The same is true today, as people receive or reject the Lord Jesus and His proclamation of liberty.

10

Remembering All the Way

Deuteronomy 8:2 And you shall remember all the way which the Lord your God has led you in the wilderness these forty years, that He might humble you, testing you, to know what was in your heart, whether you would keep His commandments or not.
Read all of Deuteronomy 8.

Thanksgiving is a time of remembering. The tradition of Thanksgiving has always been to take time out to remember God's care and provision for us and thank Him. The Pilgrims celebrated the first Thanksgiving in Plymouth, Massachusetts in 1621. They remembered and gave thanks. They remembered the Mayflower voyage, which brought them to a new home. They remembered the hard winter of 1620, which took the lives of half of their group. They remembered the good spring and good harvest of 1621. They remembered the peace they had attained with the Indians. They remembered all the trials as well as the good things and gave thanks to the Lord. They remembered *all* the way that God had led them. The Pilgrims followed the scriptural pattern of thanksgiving. They not only looked forward to their promising future, but they looked backward with thanksgiving.

The scriptural pattern of thanksgiving is seen in Deuteronomy 8 as it was given to Israel long ago. The setting was the east side of the Jordan River with the people of Israel preparing to enter Palestine. God had forged Israel in the furnace of Egypt into a nation. The Lord led His people out of that land of bondage and through the wilderness toward the promised land. Israel was delayed from entering Palestine because of unbelief and rebellion, and the people wandered in the wilderness for forty long years. In Deuteronomy 8, the people of Israel were finally on the threshold of their new home. Amid all the excitement and preparation for crossing the Jordan River, the people were given a few solemn sermons. Those sermons are what Deuteronomy is all about! The words were spoken by Moses, but they came directly from the Lord. Israel was commanded never to forget the past in looking toward the future. When the people entered and experienced the blessings of the new land (vv. 7-9), they were always to remember thankfully all the way the Lord had led them (vv. 10-18).

The growing Christian is still to follow the scriptural pattern of thanksgiving. We are to remember *all* the way the Lord has led us. We are not only to experience what the Lord is doing for us in the present and look forward with anticipation to what He has for us in the future, but we are to remember His ways with us in the past. And the implication of Deuteronomy 8 and the rest of Scripture is that we are always to remember with thanksgiving (see Ephesians 5:20, Philippians 4:6, and 1 Thessalonians 5:18). Is it possible to give thanks without remembering? Is it right to remember without giving thanks? All Christians should take time out (often) to remember with thanks *all* the way God has led.

We are to remember our *beginnings.* In verse 14 we see that the Israelites were not to forget their deliverance from slavery in the land of Egypt. They were to remember their miraculous beginnings—their exodus from more than four hundred years in bondage—the providential leadership of Moses—the plagues that God brought upon their slave-masters—the crossing of the Red Sea and the drowning of Pharoah's army. Without the gracious and sovereign intervention of the Lord, they were a doomed people. The people of Israel were expected to remember always the God of their beginnings and to give thanks.

Like Israel, growing Christians are not to forget their roots. Let us not forget how God brought us out of darkness and death into light and life (see Ephesians 2:1-5 and 1 Peter 2:9). Think of the intricate web of circumstances and experiences (even unpleasant ones) that God wove together to bring us to salvation in Christ. Let us remember to thank the Lord specifically for Christian parents or faithful Sunday school teachers or Christian friends that God used in our beginnings. When was the last time you thanked God specifically for a person He used in your beginnings as a Christian? We should not just pray for present problems or future plans. Every Christian is commanded to remember the God of our beginnings with thanksgiving.

We are also to remember our *blessings*. Israel was not only to think of all the blessings to come (Deuteronomy 8:7-9); they were to remember the blessings of the past in the wilderness (vv. 3-4). For forty years the Lord had supernaturally provided for His people. He literally sent them bread from heaven and water from rocks. He kept their clothes and sandals from wearing out for forty years (Deuteronomy 29:5)! Talk about miracles! The Lord used those blessings to humble and test His people, as we'll discuss below, but they were blessings nonetheless. (See Nehemiah 9:20-21 in this connection.) Israel was to remember all those blessings of the past and give thanks.

Do we remember to thank the Lord for all of His past blessings? Or are we too busy to remember? "Bless the

Lord, O my soul, and forget not all His benefits" (Psalm 103:2). We have a responsibility to take time out to reflect on how the Lord has blessed us, and then to thank Him specifically for all of those blessings. This should not be a thirty second ritualistic "thanks for good health and good weather" prayer. Have we ever thanked the Lord for the blessing of living in a country where we can openly buy a Bible and read it? Have we ever given thanks for the fact that we are probably more blessed with food and clothes and leisure time than over 3 billion other people? A little reflection will not only result in thanks to the Lord but may change our whole outlook and life-style before the Lord. Have we ever told the Lord how thankful we are that He has preserved and protected us from the crime and corruption in this world? And what about our spiritual blessings? Read Ephesians 1:3-14, and see how many spiritual blessings you've forgotten to thank the Lord for recently! As the old hymn says, "Count your blessings—name them one by one, And it will surprise you what the Lord has done."

Finally, we are to remember our *beatings*. Now the word "beatings" was chosen not only because it begins with the letter *b* for the alliterated outline, but because it conveys the idea of discipline. God does not vent His wrath on us with a club or whip, or anything like that, but He does discipline us as sons (Deuteronomy 8:5). Our heavenly Father disciplines us out of love, and sometimes that discipline must come by way of a beating (see Hebrews 12:5-11, particularly verse 6). Israel certainly received more than a few slaps on the wrist out there in the wilderness!

Even the way God provided for His people in the wilderness was a form of discipline, as Deuteronomy 8:5 tells us. The *way* in which God led Israel was purposely designed to humble them and test them and expose their hearts (v. 2). He let them get hungry and thirsty. Why?

He wanted to cause them to look to and depend on Him and to learn that physical food is not sufficient for life— not without a constant diet of spiritual food—the Word of God (v. 3).

Although the Lord purposely let His people get hungry and thirsty, He did not let them die of starvation or dehydration. He fed them with manna from heaven and water from flint rock (vv. 3, 15-16). Notice that it was not home-baked bread or water from wells which *they* had dug. No! It was bread from heaven and water from a most unlikely source—hard solid rock! Why? To force them to realize that, although God was humbling them and testing them, *He* was caring for them and *He* was providing for them and *He* was thinking of the best for them in the end (v. 16). But He was doing it in such a way that they could never say (even when they had inherited all the wealth of the promised land) that they had pulled off the Exodus and the "wilderness march" and the conquest by their own power and strength (vv. 17-18). Yes, Israel was to remember *all* the way the Lord had led them— especially the discipline.

Like the children of Israel, we growing Christians have to be disciplined constantly (even a few spankings!) in order to shape up and look up! The Lord purposely permits hard times "in the wilderness" to humble and test us and to discover what is in our hearts—not just what is in our heads! Hard financial times or hard family times or hard "failure" times can all be used of God to humble us and force us to look to Him in dependence. The Lord cares, and He does provide for all that we need—not necessarily all that we want! He fed Israel with manna—not steak. He gave them long-lasting clothes— not the latest styles. He took them through the great and terrible wilderness with its snakes and scorpions (v. 15)— not along the Mediterranean beaches! So the Lord deals with us in discipline. Many times His discipline is unpleasant and not easy to take (Hebrews 12:11) and often misunderstood, but our best interests are always in view (v. 16 and Hebrews 12:10). Because of that we are to remember with thanksgiving our beatings.

This Thanksgiving, let us remember *all* the way the Lord has led us.

WINTER

11

One Link in the Chain

John 4:34-38 Jesus said to them, "My food is to do the will of Him who sent Me, and to accomplish His work. Do you not say, 'There are yet four months, and then comes the harvest'? Behold, I say to you, lift up your eyes, and look on the fields, that they are white for harvest. Already he who reaps is receiving wages, and is gathering fruit for life eternal; that he who sows and he who reaps may rejoice together. For in this case the saying is true, 'One sows, and another reaps.' I sent you to reap that for which you have not labored, and you have entered into their labor."

A chain cannot be used to push, but it can be used to pull or draw. In that sense, a chain is a striking object lesson of the process by which God brings a person to Himself. God's practice is not to clobber a person into submission and then force him to walk at bayonet point to the cross. No! God's way of operation is to draw a person to Himself by a chain of love—a series of linked events and encounters that have been forged in the eternal workshop of God. The chains that God makes may take on some unexpected patterns (chains are flexible, remember), but they all lead to Him—one link at a time.

God uses a variety of links in His love chains, but the most frequent link by far is the "person link." Looking back over the chain, a new Christian will almost always be able to recall several links.

I just couldn't get that guy who was always talking about Jesus off my mind. How could I not read that little booklet he gave to me? And then there was that girl who was really concerned that I didn't have a job, and she said she would pray about it, of all things! Then after I suddenly got this job there was another girl that I kept meeting in the cafeteria. She would always bow her head before eating. My curiosity about this resulted in her sharing with me (out of a Bible she produced, seemingly from nowhere!) what was obviously the most exciting thing in her life. Her relationship with Jesus Christ was written all over her! And how can I ever forget the guy who picked me up when I was hitchhiking home from school last week? He certainly was no polished preacher, because he kept stumbling and stuttering and repeating himself. But for the first time in my life I began to understand that God loves me and that Jesus came to earth to die for me. Could it be true? What really blew my mind was when that same stuttering guy showed up two days later and told me that there were three other people praying for me! I couldn't resist all that love! That night, all alone, I committed my life to Jesus Christ.

The above testimony is not unusual. In fact, it's quite typical, because God loves to use "person links" in His chains *when they are available*. How many chains have you been used in? How many chains are out there waiting for your link?

In John 4:34-38 our Lord teaches us how to be links in the chains He is forming. Jesus used a cornfield in Samaria to teach His disciples the same lessons He wants us to learn. With a gesture of His outstretched hand He shifted the attention of the twelve from the cornfield to the "field" of the Samaritans who at that very moment were seen in the distance, making their way toward Him (v. 30). A Samaritan woman had become a link in the chains that were drawing those people to Jesus (v. 39). Former links had involved the hard work of the prophets. Now it was the disciples' turn to become links. "I sent you to reap that for which you have not labored" (v. 38). Their job was not to form the whole chain. The lesson of the fields was that they were sent to be one link in the chain. We too are sent to be links. We must learn the lessons that the master chain-builder would teach us.

Get aware! Verse 35 is a rebuke to all of us: "I say to you, lift up your eyes, and look on the fields." Jesus commands us to see the opportunities that are staring us right in the face! We're spiritually blinded so much of the time, because our interests are physical, like those of the disciples (see vv. 31-33). We are to look on the fields, not on ourselves. God is working on a lot of chains around you. In fact, there may be a loose end sitting near you right now! You may have the privilege of being the last link in the chain between that person and the Lord. On the other hand, the word you share may be just the right link now for a chain that will be completed next year. So don't be disappointed if that person doesn't become a Christian immediately. Remember, "one sows, and another reaps" (v. 37). Every link is equally important in a chain. The question remains, "Are you aware and available?"

Get busy! Our Lord's command contains urgency, because the fields are "white for harvest" (v. 35). The fruit must be picked *now!* Too often we say, "There are yet four months, and then comes the harvest" (v. 35). "After this tough semester I'll start sharing my faith." "After I get it all together *myself* I'll be ready to verbalize in the

field." Wrong thinking! The fields are ripe *now!* The
Lord is telling us that many chains out there are ready for
the last few links. Let us harvest the ripe fruit before the
frost hits!

Get crowns! The Bible speaks of reward for faithful
service and pictures it as receiving crowns (see 1 Corinthians 9:24-25). The idea here is not a selfish chalking up
of points in heaven but of living a life with eternal values
in view. There is reward both on this earth and in heaven
for faithful links according to John 4:36. Reapers who
have the privilege of being the harvest link in a chain to
eternal life draw wages even now. A million dollars can't
even begin to compare with the overwhelming joy of
leading a person to Christ! If you haven't experienced
those wages, then get out where the links are being
hooked together. Furthermore, is there any better "food"
on this earth than knowing that we are doing God's *work*
according to His *will* (v. 34)? And there is still more
reward to come! Some faithful links have not had the
chance to see the fruit of their hard work on this earth,
and we have reaped the benefits of their labor (v. 38). But
someday sower and reaper will be glad together (v. 36).
Faithful links all along the chain will celebrate together
in heaven! How many parties will you be invited to?

Question: Which link is the most important in a
chain? Answer: *Every* one! No matter how long the
chain, continuity depends on *every* link. Your link in
some chain may only be living up to what your bumper
sticker proclaims or leaving a pamphlet in a rest room,
but it could be an important link. On the other hand,
your link may be disciplined and regular prayer for a
teacher or telling the good news of Jesus Christ (even if
you stumble for words!) to a student you may not see
again after this semester. Let us take *every* opportunity to
be "one link in the chain."

12

The Road to Failure

Genesis 13:12 Abram settled in the land of Canaan, while Lot settled in the cities of the valley, and moved his tents as far as Sodom.
Read Genesis 13, 14, and 19.

High school and college students fail for a number of reasons, but one thing is common to all cases. Failure does not happen instantaneously; it is always a process. This is true of failure in the Christian life as well. Growing Christians don't suddenly "tube it." The road to failure is always a step-by-step trip.

The story of Lot in Genesis is the sad case of a believer who failed. Lot was definitely a believer. In 2 Peter 2:7-8 Lot is mentioned three times as "righteous." But righteous Lot failed to use his life for God. He traveled the road to failure. It is *possible* for *any* Christian to do the same. A Christian may either build a life that counts for God or make a shambles of his life, as far as eternal values are concerned (1 Corinthians 3:11-15). How tragic and shameful it will be for a Christian to stand before the Lord and give account for an empty and wasted life (2 Corinthians 5:10). Although that kind of failure does not determine a heaven or hell destiny for the true Christian, there are a number of warning passages in Scripture that should cause the disobedient believer to seriously question his commitment and make sure of his salvation. (See John 15:4-6 and Colossians 1:23, for example.) Let us, as growing Christians, make every effort to avoid the road to failure.

Lot's first step toward failure came because he looked at things from the *wrong perspective*. He made a selfish choice—"chose for himself" (13:11). His choice was based only on what looked like the best deal—"Lot . . . saw all the valley of the Jordan, that it was well watered everywhere" (13:10). His viewpoint did not take into account the fact that the wicked cities of the valley were programmed for destruction—"this was before the Lord destroyed Sodom and Gomorrah" (13:10). Lot had the wrong perspective, because he was not in communion with God. The viewpoint of any Christian who is out of fellowship with the Lord is the same—selfish, secular, and short-sighted.

Like Lot, many Christians start down the road to failure when they see all the possibilities and opportunities this world has to offer. It's only natural to opt for what will bring *me* the most pleasure or possessions or power. But that is the wrong perspective. God's Word states that this world and all it has to offer is doomed (see 1 Corinthians 7:31 and 1 John 2:17). Like Sodom and Gomorrah, this world is programmed for God's judgment. It is only a matter of time before the earth itself will be destroyed and replaced with "new heavens and a new earth, in which righteousness dwells" (2 Peter 3:13). No Christian in his right mind would "buy stock" in this present world system. Would you put money in a bank that you definitely knew would fail tomorrow? Would you buy a house below a dam that the authorities said was about to collapse? Of course not, but that illustrates essentially what some Christians are doing with their lives because of a worldly and natural perspective. They are investing their time and energies in something that is going to be wiped out completely and has *no* eternal value. A Christian with the wrong perspective is well on his way to a life of failure.

What a contrast we see between Lot and Abraham. Abraham was a faithful believer who had the right perspective. Abraham was in communion with God. Although Abraham and Lot had the same biological heritage, social background, and cultural surroundings (see Genesis 11 and 12), Abraham had a very different outlook on things because he walked with the Lord. Notice in Genesis 13:4-5 how Abram (God later changed his name to Abraham) worshiped the Lord when they came to the altar of Bethel. Lot was a believer also, but we don't read that Lot worshiped or called on the Lord. We only read that "Lot also had flocks and herds and tents!" What about us? Do we come at life with an Abraham perspective or a Lot perspective? In Hebrews 11:10 we are told that Abraham was "looking for the city which has foundations, whose architect and builder is God." Abraham had the right perspective. He was resting by faith on the promises of God's word to him (Genesis 12:1-3). Abraham was not interested in earthly man-made cities like Sodom and Gomorrah. He was concerned with more solid foundations—the eternal values of God. What kind of city are we looking for?

Lot's second step on the road to failure is seen in Genesis 13:12. Lot "moved his tents as far as Sodom." He didn't move into Sodom—yet! He just *flirted with the world*—usually the next step in a Christian's failure. At that point it's never a matter of living in open sin. It's just a move in the wrong direction. Taking on a good-paying job that involves you in unethical practices—getting involved in exciting extracurricular activities that take your time and talent away from the obvious needs of

the Christian group on campus—falling in love with an
"irresistible" unbeliever—all of those can be "innocent"
moves in the wrong direction. As in Lot's case, it is only a
matter of time before the failing Christian "moves into
Sodom." Before long, Lot was living in Sodom (Genesis
14:12).

Again, what a contrast we see in Abraham. In Genesis
13:18 we see that he also moved his tent, but not in the
direction of Sodom. He moved to Hebron in the high
country, and "there he built an altar to the Lord." There
was no altar near Sodom! And we also read that the Lord
promised the whole land to Abraham (13:14-17). What a
lesson! God's Word states emphatically that the Lord
Jesus is going to return some day and set up His kingdom
on this earth (2 Timothy 4:1). Faithful and enduring
Christians in *this* life are promised an abundant share in
that kingdom (see 2 Timothy 2:12; James 2:5; 2 Peter 1:5-
11). Let us not lose our reward.

In Genesis 14 we see that because of Lot's association
with Sodom, the problems of that wicked city became
Lot's problems. Abraham, on the other hand, was free
from all the turmoil, strife, and hassles of Sodom. Not
free, of course, to be unconcerned. Abraham was very
concerned about the hurts of the people of Sodom, particularly about the condition of his fellow-believer and
close relative, Lot. And he did something about it! Here
again we have a lesson about the Christian's proper
relationship to this world. A godly walk will deliver us
from much of the turmoil and confusion of this world
system (praise the Lord!), but we do have a responsibility
to help the *people* who are caught in its clutches. And we
should do everything in our power (His power!) to rescue
our failing brothers and sisters in Christ.

Like Abraham, we do not have to become part of the
"Sodom system" in order to help the people there. We're
free to help, precisely because we're *not* part of that

system. Our Lord Jesus said we were to be in contact with the world but not part of the evil world system (John 17:9-23). Notice that Abraham did not get taken in by the king of Sodom and the spoils of victory (Genesis 14:21-24). It wasn't by chance, though, that the godly Melchizedek came along just then to bless and encourage Abraham. God always has His ways of strengthening us at crucial times.

By Genesis 19 we see that Lot is fully *ensnared* in the affairs of Sodom. Again that is but another logical step on the road to failure. We would think that Lot would have learned his lesson from his narrow escape in chapter 14, or at least from the love that Abraham had demonstrated for him. But failing believers become hardened to love and common sense. Imagine Abraham's discouragement. Many of us can identify with Abraham at this point. Sometimes it takes a very earth-shaking and traumatic event to get a believer out of Sodom. A visit from angels and fire from heaven finally forced Lot from Sodom, but even then it was not without great struggle, procrastination, and loss (19:15-29). Lot's reluctance to leave is not the only indication that he was ensnared in Sodom. A close study of these chapters indicates that Lot probably married a woman of Sodom. He got rid of his tent and bought a permanent house in Sodom. He raised his family in Sodom, and family roots are hard to sever.

Furthermore, it seems that Lot may have been entangled in the political corruption of Sodom. The expression "sitting in the gate of Sodom" (19:1) can mean that he was involved in the business affairs of Sodom. Now it *may* have been that Lot was trying to bring about city reform, but it is very interesting that Abraham, from outside the city, was more of a testimony to the people and the king of Sodom in one day than Lot was in a lifetime inside the city. Like Lot, the ensnared Christian may not be involved in the "grosser" sins of this world like homosexuality and violence (19:2-9), but his thinking becomes twisted and distorted (19:8), because he is out of touch with God. And any little vestige of testimony is ignored and mocked (19:14). A failing Christian at that stage is a sorry sight.

The final scene we have of Lot is tragic. By the mercy of God his life was preserved but he lost everything—job, home, possessions, wife. It is true that Lot was able to take his two daughters out of Sodom, but he was not able to take Sodom out of his daughters (19:30-38). From those incestuous relationships came Moab and Ammon—nations that were to plague the people of God for years to come. Lot's failure, which began with a choice, had disastrous effects upon himself, his family, and all of Israel. The story of Lot is a clear and solemn warning for every growing Christian. Don't travel the road to failure!

13

Hope That Will Not Disappoint

Romans 5:5-8 And hope does not disappoint, because the love of God has been poured out within our hearts through the Holy Spirit who was given to us. For while we were still helpless, at the right time Christ died for the ungodly. For one will hardly die for a righteous man; though perhaps for a good man someone would dare even to die. But God demonstrates His own love toward us, in that while we were yet sinners, Christ died for us.

Have you ever really thought about the words of the familiar Christmas carols that we sing year after year? Listen to these words from "O Little Town of Bethlehem": "The hopes and fears of all the years Are met in thee tonight." What hopes and fears of man were met in Bethlehem on that first Christmas night? The age-old fears of mankind could all be summed up in the question, "Is there someone out there to whom man has to answer?" The hopes of the years were centered in the longing to know that there was Someone out there who cared! The birth of Jesus in Bethlehem brought an end to the fears and gave substance to the hopes of mankind.

But how do we know that we are not just "whistling in the dark up a blind alley?" How do we really know that the Christian hope in Jesus Christ will not disappoint us or deceive us or delude us in the end? The answer to that question is what Romans 5:5-8 is all about. That Scripture tells us that we can be sure that our hope will not disappoint us in the end. There are two sides to the argument used to drive home the truth. Let's call them the personal, or subjective, side and the historical, or objective, side.

The personal side of the argument is contained in verse 5: "Because the love of God has been poured out within our hearts through the Holy Spirit who was given to us." The Spirit of God has made His permanent home within every Christian. What is He doing there? He is imparting the love of God to us. Does the "love of God" mean our love toward God or God's love toward us? (Think before you answer.) It can mean both! The Holy Spirit pours out the love of God by communicating God's love to us and producing our love for God.

The best evidence that God's love has been communicated to us is not a "warm feeling" inside or a "spiritual high" at camp last summer or an ecstatic experience somewhere along the line, but the fact that we actually love God! Think back on your closest moment with the Lord. The evidence that you were sensing the flood of God's love was your response, "O Lord, I love You."

Only a true Christian has love for God! Others may have a healthy respect for Him. They may try to "chalk up points" with Him. They may even try to defend Him. However, the "fears of all the years" are really still there. But when a person actually loves God, it is evidence that something unique has happened. Do you love God?

The historical side of the argument is found in verse 6 and following. There *was* a man named Jesus born into history at Bethlehem about two thousand years ago. That

He claimed to be the Christ and the hope of all mankind cannot be denied even by His critics. That He was a man among men and went about doing good is authenticated. That He had supernatural power and was resurrected from the dead has ample evidence that no skeptic has ever been able to dismiss. And that He willingly gave up His life for His enemies is also historical fact—but hard to explain by the nonbeliever. Has anyone else in history ever done that?

Soldiers have been known to die for their close buddies. Mothers have given their lives for their children. It is always an extremely rare case when one person gives his life for another person—even when that person is a really nice guy (verse 7). But Jesus Christ voluntarily died for the *ungodly* (verse 6)!

Christ was born to die. The first Christmas anticipated Good Friday. It was not by chance that our Lord went to the cross. It was God's appointed and fixed time—"at the right time" (verse 6). The Lord Jesus foretold His own death when He said, "For even the Son of Man did not come to be served, but to serve, and to give His life a ransom for many" (Mark 10:45). That is why Jesus voluntarily gave up His life. He died for *us!* "While we were yet sinners, Christ died for us" (Romans 5:8). Here is objective proof (proof that doesn't depend on our experience) that God loves us and our hope in Him is not in vain.

The next time you're "down" and wishing you could feel more of the love of God, think about how God demonstrated His love. Look *out*, to what God has done in history for you. Looking *in* at your own feelings can be very disappointing. The Lord Jesus died for us, whether we feel it or not! It is historical proof that the Christian hope is not a hoax.

On Christmas morning there will be a few disappointed children. A particular gift they had hoped for will not be

under the tree. How different is the Christian hope in the
Lord Jesus Christ! We have a hope that *will not* disappoint us in the end. Praise God!

14

True Christmas Spririt

Philippians 2:5-8 Your attitude should be the same as that of Christ Jesus: Who, being in very nature God, did not consider equality with God something to be grasped, but made himself nothing, taking the very nature of a servant, being made in human likeness. And being found in appearance as a man, he humbled himself and became obedient to death— even death on a cross (NIV).
Read Philippians 2:1-11.

Getting the Christmas spirit means different things to different people. To some, it is that beautiful warm feeling of "no place like home for the holidays." To others, it is the excitement of shopping for gifts and wrapping them by the tree. To the student, the Christmas spirit is getting away from school and studies for a while. In other words, to get psyched up for the good things to come at Christmas is to catch the proverbial spirit of Christmas.

But what about Christ? Isn't He part of the spirit of Christmas? Not really! Except for a few token nativity scenes, our society has pretty much removed the Lord Jesus from Christmas. Christmas has become so secularized within our culture that a person can fully catch the "Christmas spirit" without having a single meaningful thought of Jesus.

The true spirit of Christmas, of course, gives Christ His rightful place. That does not mean more manger scenes and sacred carols—it means more of the mind and attitude of Christ. To catch the true Christmas spirit is to be characterized more by the self-giving spirit of the Lord. That is hardly possible for a nonbelieving, non-Christian world—even at Christmastime. But it is possible for the growing Christian, because the life of Christ is there, empowered by the Holy Spirit. Philippians 2:5-8 tells us that it is the Christian's responsibility to let the mind or attitude of the Lord Jesus be reproduced in us and characterize us. To have the attitude of self-denial and self-sacrifice is to have the mind of Christ. That is the true and biblical Christmas spirit.

The reason for the writing of this great doctrinal passage of Scripture was a common problem in the Christian church. Many of the Philippians were being selfish and proud and looking out only for themselves (2:3-4). Sound familiar? The Philippian problem is always a contemporary problem. The priority of self always seems to be at the top of the list. No wonder God chose to include the letter of the apostle Paul to the Philippians as part of His Holy Word. That is the word of the Lord to us today as much as it was to the Philippian believers. Let us hear it!

We are to exhibit more togetherness and love for one another (2:2). To do our own thing and be independent from the other believers of the fellowship is not scriptural. We are to look out for the interests of our brothers and sisters (2:3-4). To ignore or put down other members of the Christian community is not scriptural. We are to reach out and love brothers and sisters with whom we find it hard to get along (2:2; see also 4:2). We are to strive for unity of mind and spirit and purpose with those fellow-believers who do not see everything exactly our way (2:2; see also 1:27). It is not easy, but it is scriptural. The true spirit of Christmas involves a lot of self-denying and self-sacrificing and self-giving.

The supreme illustration of what it means to give of oneself in the interests of others is the example of the eternal Son of God. He gave up the glory and majesty of heaven—for us (2:6). He identified with the human predicament by becoming man—for us (v. 7). He voluntarily gave up His hold on life and died—for us (v. 8). Every step of the path of our Lord was a further surrender of what was His by right. That is the mind or attitude that is to characterize the Christian. How can I push for my own "rights" after reading such a Scripture? Having the true spirit of Christmas is a far cry from having the "Christmas spirit"!

As mentioned above, this portion of the Word of God has great doctrinal significance. Contained in these few short verses is the doctrine of the incarnation. God became man; surely, this is the story of Christmas. Because this Scripture has often been misunderstood, it is important that we examine the verses closely. The first phrase of verse 6 tells us that Jesus did not *begin* being God at Bethlehem, and He did not *stop* being God at Bethlehem. "Being in very nature God" conveys the idea of always having been and being God. As an illustration, we could say of Bruce Jenner, the 1976 Olympic decathlon champion: "Jenner, being in very nature an athlete, won the gold medal at Montreal." Jenner did not become an athlete at Montreal; he was an athlete long before, and he still is an athlete—in his very nature or "essence."

Because the eternal Son was God in the very essence of His being, He had all the external manifestations or effects or equalities of deity. There was no glory or majesty of God that was not His. The second phrase of

verse 6 begins to show us the marvelous self-giving attitude of God. The eternal Son did not consider those
external manifestations of deity something He had to
grasp or hold onto like a treasure. He put aside those
glories (but not His essence!) in order to come to us! The
word "equality" in the phrase "equality with God" is
really the plural, "equalities." It means the outward
signs or manifestations of being equal with God. The
insignia of deity were voluntarily laid aside by the Son of
God when He came to earth.

He emptied Himself (v. 7). The eternal Son never
emptied Himself of His deity, but only of the outward
manifestations of that deity. When coming to this planet
He stripped Himself of His heavenly glory and majesty.
There was no Christmas card halo around the head of
that perfect Baby in Bethlehem's manger. But what about
His divine attributes—His being omnipotent (having all
power), omniscient (having all knowledge), and omnipresent (being present in all places)? Did the Son of God
empty Himself of those qualities when He came into this
world? No! Those attributes are inherent in the very
nature and essence of God, and in no way did the *eternal*
Son stop being God at the incarnation. The Lord Jesus
voluntarily gave up the use of His divine attributes for
Himself, but He did not empty Himself of them.

Throughout the gospel record we catch glimpses of
our Lord using His divine attributes in the interest of
others. His omnipotence gave Him power over disease
when He healed the sick, over death when He raised the
dead to life, over the demonic beings when He exorcized
demons, and over disaster when He calmed the sea. (See
Luke 8 for all four in one chapter.) Our Lord's omniscience
gave Him foreknowledge of the exact details that were to
take place in His future—His suffering, His rejection,
His death, His resurrection (Mark 8:31). He knew who

would betray Him (Matthew 26:21-25). He knew Peter would deny Him exactly three times before dawn (Mark 14:29-30). He knew His death would be by crucifixion (John 12:32-33). He knew His ascension would follow His resurrection (John 14:28-29).

What about the Lord's omnipresence while He was here on this earth? Although that concept stretches our finite minds, the Scripture indicates that even that attribute was not given up at the incarnation. Take, for example, Matthew 18:20 where Jesus said, "Where two or three have gathered together in My name, there I am in their midst." Although that statement is usually applied to His presence among us now, let us remember that He said it in the present tense *then*—while He was bodily here on earth. Of course the body of our Lord was in only one place at one time, as is His resurrected body now. If we strip the Son of God of His omnipresence because He took on a body at the incarnation, we deny Him an essential part of His deity forever—because Jesus lives today, bodily! We will see our Lord Jesus in *Person* someday, and yet He is in our midst now. He is omnipresent. The eternal Son has always been omnipresent. The Christian doctrine of the omnipresence of God is: *All* of God in *all* places at *all* times.

Verse 7 indicates that at the incarnation the Son of God took "the very nature of a servant, being made in human likeness." The point here is that God took on manhood. Notice the link with the beginning of verse 6. He always had the very nature of God (v. 6), but He took the very nature of man (v. 7). The idea is not that He gave up one nature to take on another nature, but rather that He took on the nature of man in addition to His being God. Jesus was, and is, fully God and fully man. He is not 50 percent God and 50 percent man; He is 100 percent God and 100 percent man! The Son took on "the very nature of a servant" and surrendered Himself totally to the will of the Father (Matthew 20:28). "Being made in human likeness" means that He was a real and genuine man with all the essential attributes of humanity—except for the sinful nature, of course (see 2 Corinthians 5:21; 1 John 3:5; 1 Peter 2:22). But the expression "human *likeness*" further implies that He was not simply and merely man—it safeguards His continued deity; He was the incarnate Son of God.

There was nothing unusual about our Lord's appearance when He walked on this planet. "Being found in appearance as a man" (v. 8) means that He ate and spoke and dressed like the men of that generation and culture. He was like a king who takes off his royal robes temporarily, and puts on the clothes of a peasant to identify and empathize with his people. The Lord's glory and majesty and kingship were veiled.

As the perfect man and Servant, Jesus gave obediently of Himself for others to the point of death by crucifixion (v. 8). That is the mind or attitude that is to characterize the growing Christian—the true Christmas spirit.

15

Christian Giving is More Than Christmas Giving

2 Corinthians 8:9 For you know the grace of our Lord Jesus Christ, that though He was rich, yet for your sake He became poor, that you through His poverty might become rich.
Read all of 2 Corinthians 8.

We all know that the true spirit of Christmas is "not getting, but giving." Our experience proves that there really is more joy in giving than in receiving Christmas gifts. (That *is* your experience, isn't it?) But even so, much of our Christmas giving tends to fall short of true Christian giving. For one thing, Christmas giving usually doesn't cost us all that much, and furthermore, a Christmas gift usually doesn't help to meet someone's true needs. But true Christian giving is different—it goes so much farther. How far? Christian giving goes to the point where it begins to *"hurt"* the giver and really *help* the receiver. Have you done any real Christian giving lately?

Scattered throughout the eighth chapter of 2 Corinthians are seven principles of Christian giving. The church in Jerusalem was very poor at that time. The apostle Paul, in his missionary travels, was taking up a collection

85

for the Christians in Jerusalem from various churches in
the Mediterranean world. The churches from Macedonia
(northern part of modern Greece) had already given very
generously (vv. 1-2). Now Paul was urging the Christians
at Corinth (central part of modern Greece) to follow the
example of the Macedonian Christians and to complete
the collection they had begun the year before (vv. 6, 10-11,
and 24). From Paul's message to the Corinthians in this
chapter emerge seven principles to help growing Christians to become giving Christians.

The first principle is primary to all Christian giving:
Give yourself first (v. 5). The Macedonians first gave their
own *selves*, then gave their own *substance*. If I am not
really "into" my giving, it is not true Christian giving.
After all, the Lord doesn't really need my substance or my
service. He could have money grow on trees and have
angels do all the work! But He wants *me*. Notice (v. 5) the
direction that such giving of ourselves is to take—"to the
Lord and to us." Some Christians have the idea that, if
they run off and live in seclusion "in dedication to the
Lord," they are giving of themselves. No way! The verti-
cal ("to the Lord") must include the horizontal ("to us")
to qualify as true Christian giving. We are to be involved
on a down-to-earth basis with *people* who have needs.
Note that that is "by the will of God" (again verse 5).

Another principle of Christian giving is: *Give to the
point of sacrifice* (v. 3). The Macedonians were not giving
the "surplus off the top" or whatever amount happened
to be left over at the end of the month! Verse 2 shows us
that those Christians were poor and under pressure to
begin with, and yet they gave in the midst of their
problems and in spite of their poverty. They gave till it
really hurt! Certainly our measly contribution of a few
dollars or an hour a week falls short of that divine
principle. How far should we carry the principle of
sacrifice? The next two principles give us guidelines.

Give after the example of our Lord (v. 9). How much did the Lord Jesus give? He gave all! And it wasn't just for His friends; He gave His whole life for His enemies and for the likes of you and me. Why? So that "you through His poverty might become rich."

But how does one give all? Should we sell all we own and go around in a pair of old jeans and a T-shirt and live in a cheap apartment? Well, that wouldn't be the worst reaction to this principle, and some of us may be called upon to live very much like that. However, Scripture is always balanced. The balancing principle here is found in verses 13-15: *Give toward equality.* Although the Macedonians were not wealthy, they did have more than those in Jerusalem at that time, and so it was right that they aim for equality. The intent was not that the Christians in Jerusalem should be eased to the point where the Corinthians would be poverty-stricken (v. 13). No, the aim was for equality. When we see others with a greater need than ourselves, we should at least make a start toward equality. Something is wrong if we are too comfortable while others are in need! Praise God for Christian organizations that are concerned about the crying needs of people around the world. We should give liberally to those organizations.

But isn't this equality principle indirectly teaching communism? No! Verse 15 guards against such thinking. Verse 15 is a quotation from the Old Testament (Exodus 16:18) in reference to the manna. Read that account of how God miraculously provided bread for His people, and it becomes clear that equality was accomplished on the basis of needs, not amount. Communism aims for equality, but it is on the basis of the same amount for everyone. Christian giving aims for equality on the basis of *meeting needs.* If we are giving toward equality, we should not have more than we need! Enough to meet our needs, yes! Huge bank accounts, no! We must deal with our hoarding tendencies before the Lord.

A fifth principle of Christian giving comes to us from verse 12: *Give willingly*. This principle of giving with desire is also emphasized in verses 3, 4, and 8. From those verses we see that Paul was not commanding them to give. It was to be totally voluntary—as a proof that their Christian love was sincere (v. 8). The Macedonians had been very willing. They actually begged Paul for the privilege of being able to share in meeting the needs of their brothers and sisters in Jerusalem. What an example to the Corinthians! What a message to us!

A further principle of Christian giving is also contained in verse 12: *Give what you have*. The point here is that the Lord does not expect us to give what we don't have, but He does expect us to give on the basis of what we have. Do you *have* the ability to work with small children (or teenagers, or home Bible studies)? How much of that ability is being given to the Lord, and how much is being left unused and undeveloped and ungiven? Do you *have* the time to talk to your lab partner (or friend at work or neighbor)? How much of that time is given to a definite attempt to reach that person with the love of Christ, and how much is being left for small talk? The Lord doesn't look so much on what we give as on what we have left!

For the final principle of Christian giving from this chapter, let us look at verse 11: *Give according to plan*. Desire is not enough in Christian giving. There must be a deliberate setting aside of time, talent, and treasure, and then an actual giving in accordance with that plan. The Corinthians were not to stop with good intentions; they were to complete what they had purposed. Many of us growing Christians have good intentions and desires in the area of Christian giving. We will say "right on!" to a devotional such as this. But we never really get out the pencil and paper, as it were, and deliberately plan how much TV and magazine time we will "sacrifice" each week in order to give of ourselves to the work of the Lord. Christian giving will never come off with desire alone. We must give according to a deliberate and studied plan.

Here, then, are a few principles of Christian giving from one chapter of God's Word. There are others, but certainly we have enough here to show us that we all need to get out that pencil and paper. Maybe New Year's Eve would be an ideal time. Between now and then let us pray that the Lord would open our eyes to the particular needs that He would have us meet with our time, our talent, or our treasure. Then let us deliberately plan how we *can* and *will* give to meet those needs—willingly and to the point of sacrifice. Yes, true Christian giving is a lot more than the usual Christmas giving.

16

Focal Points of Failure

Nehemiah 9:38 Now because of all this we are making an agreement in writing; and on the sealed document are the names of our leaders, our Levites and our priests.

Read also Nehemiah 10 and 13.

January is the month when most of our New Year's resolutions are broken. Before the very first month of the year is over, our "new start" is history. Our resolution to jog ten minutes a day has been changed to a running program of ten minutes a week! Our resolution to lose a pound a week has been rationalized to a "no gain" policy! Our resolution to get up an hour earlier each day for time alone with the Lord has been modified to a short five-minute devotional plan sometime during the day—if nothing more important comes up! As human beings we have a natural tendency to fail in whatever we set out to do. And as growing Christians we are not immune. Our well-laid plans for more discipline and efficiency in our lives as Christians often result in just that—only plans! How discouraging! What is the answer?

The answer from Scripture can be stated in the following way: 1. We don't have to fail in any point. 2. But we will fail in some points. 3. Therefore, concentrate on what may become focal points of failure. As to the first part of the answer, the Bible teaches that when a person becomes a Christian he receives brand new life in Christ (2 Corinthians 5:17). That new life is empowered by the Holy Spirit who indwells *every* believer (1 Corinthians 6:19). Thus Christians are enabled *not to sin* (Romans 6:11-14 and Romans 8:9-12). We know also from Scripture that God never permits an overwhelming test or temptation to confront a Christian. 1 Corinthians 10:13 assures us that there is never a "can't handle" situation in the life of a Christian. It may be extremely hard at times, but a Christian does not *have to* sin or fail in any particular situation.

The second part of the answer is equally true for *every* Christian. We are not perfect—yet! Most of us will not argue that point! First John 1:8-10 tells us that every Christian still sins. Although we have new life in Christ, we still struggle with sin, because sin is still at work within our mortal bodies (Romans 7:15-25). We cannot say that we are completely failure-free until we are with the Lord. *Then* we will be perfect (1 John 3:2 and Romans 8:23). In the meantime, we are to make every effort not to yield ourselves to sin (Hebrews 12:1 and Romans 6:15-19), but to yield ourselves to the Spirit of God who indwells us and empowers our new life in Christ (Galatians 5:16-18 and Romans 8:1-4). And what about the sins that we will inevitably commit? We confess them to the Lord. Confession brings sure cleansing (see 1 John 1:9 and 1 John 2:1).

The reason for the third part of the answer is a very practical one. Sin snowballs! When we fail in one area, it isn't long before other areas are affected. Therefore we should concentrate on key areas—areas that can become focal points of failure. When sin and failure take place in those areas there is a tendency to "blow it big." Sometimes a life of failure is the result. There are three basic areas in which a growing Christian should be especially committed before the Lord. Let us call them the areas of our ties, our times, and our treasure. "Ties" has to do with our relationships; "time" has to do with our priorities; "treasure" has to do with our possessions. If those basic areas do not remain focal points of commitment, they can become focal points of failure.

The Scriptures selected from the book of Nehemiah impress on us the importance of being committed in all three key areas. Nehemiah records for us the events in the history of Israel near the close of the Old Testament period. Nehemiah motivated the Jewish people who had returned to the homeland from the captivity in Babylon to rebuild the wall of Jerusalem (chapters 1-6 of Nehemiah). Upon completion of the wall, there was a time of great rejoicing and revival among God's people (chapters 7-9). The revival occurred not only because of a physical return of the people to their land but because of a spiritual return of the people to their God.

In Nehemiah 9:38 we see that the leaders of the people of God made a "New Year's resolution" to faithfully follow the Lord from that time forward. In chapter 10 we find that not only were the leaders involved, but *all* the people agreed to the terms of the resolution—even the teenagers (vv. 28-29)! As we examine the last half of chapter 10, we discover that the specific areas of commitment agreed upon were their ties (v. 30), their time (v. 31), and their treasure (vv. 32-39). When we come to chapter 13, at least twelve years had elapsed since the time of commitment. During the latter part of that time, Nehemiah was gone from Jerusalem on official business (13:6). When Nehemiah returned, things had changed, and the situation was pretty bad. The three focal points of commitment had become focal points of failure.

In Nehemiah 10:30 the people of Israel promised that they would not intermarry with their pagan neighbors.

They would remain pure in their relationships. In Nehemiah 13:23-28 we find that the people of God had broken their pledge. As a result, the children of those mixed marriages were infected with the surrounding pagan culture (v. 24). Even the high priestly family was no longer separated (v. 28).

The application of this to the growing Christian is pretty straightforward. Second Corinthians 6:14 tells us that we are not to be "unequally yoked together with unbelievers" (KJV). Marriage to an unbeliever results in all kinds of bad fallout for years to come. The home is not Christ-centered, and the children are infected with the surrounding world system.

An "unequal yoke" becomes a focal point of failure. God, in His wonderful kindness, can step into the situation and pick up the pieces, but scars can remain. God's Word is clear on the point of marriage, and it is to be obeyed. Certainly commitment in the area of our relationships or ties can be applied to areas other than marriage, but because marriage is a critical part of our lives, let us be sure we are committed at this point. If we fail here, the rest of our lives can be affected. The drastic action of Nehemiah in verse 25 forces us to realize the seriousness of such failure. The mention in verse 26 of King Solomon and his place before God should convince us that even the most mature Christian is vulnerable. Are your own ties a focal point of commitment right now?

The people pledged (Nehemiah 10:31) that they would put God first in the use of their time. Every seventh day and certain feast days would be set apart for worship and service for the Lord. Those times would not be used to buy or sell or "do their own thing"; the Lord would have top priority. In Nehemiah 13:15-22 we see that Israel failed in this area. The Sabbath day had become just like any other day. Instead of using that time to worship and serve the Lord, the people were using it for their own ends—working and buying and selling for themselves. What a reversal of priorities!

What about *our* priorities? Is God *first* in the area of our time? Let's face it. If the Lord does not have top priority, we don't give Him much time at all. Just as in Nehemiah's day, there are always plenty of activities to gobble up the Lord's time. Little by little He is squeezed out of our busy schedules. Wrong priorities become a focal point of failure. Our Lord Jesus promised that if we put God *first*, He will take care of all the really necessary things of life (Matthew 6:25-34 and especially verse 33). Our problem is that we are not content with what the Lord provides. Too much of our time is consumed with buying and selling, far more than we really need. Our priorities need to be put in order. Our time must be a focal point of commitment, because there is never any "leftover" time for the Lord.

In Nehemiah 10:32-39 the people of Israel declared that they would continually give of their possessions to support the work of the Lord. They promised to faithfully give back to the Lord a tenth of all He gave to them. Those gifts would always include the first part of the income—not whatever happened to be left of the "paycheck or allowance!" In Nehemiah 13:10-14 we find that the people of God failed in this area also. The tithes and offerings were not being brought to the Temple nor given to the priests and other servants of the Lord. The Levites, who were responsible for much of the work around the Temple, were forced back to secular employment (v. 10). Out of neglect, Israel's treasure had become a focal point of failure.

That can happen to us as well. The proper use of our "treasure" for the Lord must be a focal point of commitment. We are to be disciplined in our giving to support the Lord's work. We should follow the example given to us in 1 Corinthians 16:2. The Corinthian believers were told to put aside part of their money each week for the Lord. That is disciplined and proportionate giving, which should characterize the growing Christian in the use of *all* of his possessions. It is a cop-out for a Christian to say, "I don't give proportionately, because all I have is the Lord's!" If we don't get down to the "pencil and notebook" stage of Christian giving, it usually doesn't come off at all! It isn't long before the work of the Lord suffers somewhere. May God help us not to let our possessions become a focal point of failure.

In chapter 13 we find Nehemiah taking drastic action to correct the areas of failure. This adds to the beautiful character description we have of Nehemiah, and teaches us that we may have to take drastic action to shape up in the three basic areas of commitment. Before the first month of the year is over we'll probably fail in a few of our little New Year's resolutions. Let's concentrate on keeping the three "biggies" from becoming points of failure.

17

Total Commitment

Luke 5:3-5   And He got into one of the boats, which was Simon's, and asked him to push out a little way from the land. And He sat down and began teaching the multitudes from the boat. And when He had finished speaking, He said to Simon, "Put out into the deep water and let down your nets for a catch." And Simon answered and said, "Master, we worked hard all night and caught nothing, but at your bidding I will let down the nets."
Read the whole account in Luke 5:1-11.

We say we are committed to the Lord Jesus Christ. How committed? Total commitment means that Jesus Christ is Lord in every area of our lives. He must be Lord on Saturday night as well as Sunday morning. He must be Lord of our bodies as well as our brains. He must be Lord of what we save as well as what we sacrifice. He must be Lord of our careers as well as our creed. Are we totally committed to Jesus Christ? Is He Lord of all?

As recorded at the beginning of Luke 5, Peter was up on the beach washing his fishing nets. When we come to verse 11, we see that Peter had left his boat and his nets and everything to follow the Lord. The miracle of the great catch of fish resulted in a miracle in the life of Peter. Peter's steps toward total commitment are steps that growing Christians must take as well.

The first step is *getting involved.* Peter was *willing* to let Jesus use his boat. Luke 4:38 indicates that Peter already knew the Lord at that time, but until then he had been content just to hear the Word of God while continuing his normal way of living (5:1-2). What a picture of a lot of Christians! Know the Lord? Yes! Willing to listen to the Word of God? Yes! Changing their life-styles? No! In fact, from their lives, it is hard to tell them from non-Christians, trying to get ahead in this world (of all things) and "washing their nets" (5:1) for a bigger catch, just barely within hearing distance of the Lord.

Then Peter took a step in the right direction. He turned his boat over to the Lord. We too must be willing to turn over what we own to the Lord for His use. We own things, time, talent. Are we willing to share the cassette tapes and books that have been such a help to us? Are we willing to turn over our homes to the Lord—including the cherished furniture that could take a beating from those who need to meet the Lord? Are we willing to *make* time available for the Lord's use? What about that student in need of love who keeps disrupting schedules and draining away precious study time? Are we willing to invest our abilities and talents and gifts, or should we go on hoarding them? Are our athletic abilities, for example, available in some way for the Lord to use, or do we use them only to bring glory to ourselves? It is hypocrisy to speak of total commitment to the Lord when we are not willing to turn over our "boats" to Him.

The next step the Lord wants us to make toward total commitment is to *push out a little* (v. 3). It is one thing to take what we own and make it available for the Lord's use, but it is another thing to step out a little by faith from the "security of the land." Let us not only open our rooms or homes for a Bible study—let us actually start one! Let us not only make our weekends available for the Lord—let's actually take on a Sunday school class! Yes, it takes faith—there is risk and sacrifice involved, but that's what pushing out from land is all about.

The Lord Jesus did not force Peter; He asked him (v. 3). The Lord could have simply walked out on the water without the use of any boat. But He didn't. He wanted Peter to get involved in the action. He chose to teach the people out of Peter's boat. God delights to use us for His glory if we just step out a little bit by faith. But we love the security of the land. We are reluctant to move away from shore. How can we talk about total commitment to Jesus Christ if we are not willing to push out a little?

Peter was told to take a final step of total commitment—to *launch out* into the deep (v. 4). Here one finds total dependence on the Lord. No more land or shallow water! Commitment is no longer a sideline. In many ways it is the "point of no return." My education and career are no longer planned with "land" in view. My field of work and study are determined by God's will for my life. It is no longer a question of what field will give me the greatest return or security or peace or chance for advancement in this world. It is now a matter of subjecting my education, my career, my choice of life partner, my *all* to the lordship of Christ. Am I still playing at token efforts in the shallow water of Christian commitment, or have I launched out into the deep?

It is in the deep that we experience the Lord's power. We learn that He really does provide in a miraculous way for the very needs that may have held us back from total commitment! We may work all night to make it in this life and still catch nothing (v. 5), but the person who is totally committed to the Lord does not worry about the needs of this life. If he seeks first the kingdom of God and His righteousness, then he knows that those things will be provided (Matthew 6:33).

It is in the deep that we learn to worship. Jesus is no longer just "a Friend invited into my life." He is God! When Peter experienced the Lord's power in the deep he was not only amazed (v. 9), but he fell down before Jesus and confessed, "I am a sinful man, O Lord" (v. 8). The more committed we are to Jesus Christ, the more we are aware of our sinfulness and His holiness. What a blessing to know that the Lord Jesus does not depart from us but comforts us and transforms us. "Do not fear, from now on you will be catching men" (v. 10).

Peter left everything and followed his Lord. Yes, there were failures yet to come in Peter's life. Total commitment does not mean perfection. It's a matter of taking *self* off every throne of life and enthroning *Christ*. How committed are you to Jesus Christ? Have you launched out into the deep, or are you still hung up on the beach? Total commitment means Jesus Christ is Lord of all.

18

Seven Thousand Knees
and Mouths

1 Kings 19:18   Yet I will leave 7,000 in Israel, all the knees that have not bowed to Baal and every mouth that has not kissed him.
Read all of 1 Kings 16-19.

What's so significant about seven thousand pairs of knees and seven thousand mouths? The significance lies not in what the knees and mouths *did*, but rather in what they *did not* do. The knees did not bow down to any of the heathen gods named Baal, and the mouths did not kiss any image of Baal. Romans 15:4 assures us that there is a lesson here for our benefit: "For whatever was written in earlier times was written for our instruction, that through perseverance and the encouragement of the Scriptures we might have hope."

Let's back up a bit and take a quick look at the historical setting in which the faithful knees and mouths were situated. (Read all of 1 Kings 16-19.) At that particular point in Israel's history, it was not exactly popular to be a believer in the Lord God! Notorious King Ahab and wicked Queen Jezebel ruled the land. The country was given over to immorality and idolatry. Religious prostitution accompanied the pagan worship of Baal.

Many true prophets had been openly murdered by Jezebel's forces. No public outcry was being voiced by any group within the nation. In fact, an individual risked his life if he spoke out against the corrupt conditions.

It was against that dark background that the prophet Elijah burst upon the scene with dramatic suddenness and announced judgment. He dared to speak out publicly against the moral and spiritual decay that was overrunning the country. He preached his fiery sermon of judgment to the king himself. God miraculously protected and preserved and provided for His faithful and courageous prophet. God has many ways of taking care of His children who are willing to stand up and speak out against sin—even today, and even you! Elijah fearlessly forced the prophets of Baal into a major showdown between their gods and the God of Israel. There at Mount Carmel, in an awe-inspiring display of power, the Lord showed Himself unquestionably supreme over Baal and the pagan prophets. Many of the prophets of Baal were seized and eliminated. The Lord sent a long-delayed rain as a sign of His blessing. For a few fleeting hours, it looked like the country was on the verge of a national revival.

But revival did not come. In fact, Elijah himself was now running scared. Queen Jezebel had personally threatened his life because of his actions at Mount Carmel. For the first time, we read that Elijah was afraid (19:3). If a great prophet of God like Elijah could so quickly lose his determination and courage, what does that say about us? Let us remember that we are not immune to such a comedown. Our strong witness and faith is no guarantee that we are invulnerable to events that could bring about a quick downfall. We must constantly depend upon the Lord for *His* strength and *His* courage.

Elijah hightailed it as fast as he could to the extreme southern end of the country and beyond—all the way to

Mount Horeb in the Sinai Peninsula. Here, far from Jezebel's clutches, he struggled with God. Elijah was convinced that he was the only faithful believer left in Israel (19:10, 14).

Have you ever felt the same way? You've tried so hard to serve the Lord, but you just don't seem to get any support. For a brief moment, things seem to be looking up; then the bottom falls out again. Those who call themselves your brothers and sisters in the Lord seem to disappear, just when you need their help the most. Certainly they can't be *real* Christians! You must be the only true believer on the campus of your school or in the company that employs you or even in the church you attend.

But Elijah was wrong! He was not the only one who had stayed true to the Lord. There were still seven thousand faithful men and women in Israel who had not bowed the knee to Baal nor kissed his image. The Lord's reminder of the seven thousand appears to be a mild rebuke to the prophet. Elijah may have had some good reasons for thinking that he was the only "evangelical" around, but God still had a few other faithful believers scattered throughout the country. The secret "seven thousand" still exists today. Be very careful before you jump to the conclusion that you are the only believer in your school or job or neighborhood. The Lord still has some secret believers sprinkled around.

Certainly the seven thousand secret believers should have been more outspoken and publicly supportive of Elijah's ministry. They really did have a responsibility to stand up and be counted as believers. But at least they were still hanging in there. They had not bowed their knees to Baal, and they had not kissed his image. The Lord knew them and counted them! Although they were unwilling to be counted in public, they were known by exact number to God. That should be an encouragement to us. Maybe you're the "silent Christian" type. You know you should be more outspoken about your faith. You can remember scores of occasions when you had the opportunity to say something for Christ but blew it because of fear. But at least you haven't *denied* the Lord. You don't speak His name in vain. You've resisted the temptation to "bow" to the all-too-available sex on campus. You've refused to let down the barriers and "kiss" the ungodly literature and X-rated films that pervade our culture. Take heart and be encouraged. You are one of the seven thousand.

It may be significant that 1 Kings 19:18 does not talk about the seven thousand who believed *in their hearts.* No, it is a much more objective statement. They did not *bow the knee* or *kiss the image.* God is looking for evidence in our actions for the faith that is in our hearts. You may not be an up-front and outspoken Elijah, but God still expects that evidence of your faith will be worked out in your life. God is counting on more than just a belief in the heart. Therefore, continue to resist the temptation to just believe secretly. That is one of Satan's most successful tactics in getting growing Christians to compromise—especially silent-type Christians. The fact that you may never be one of those good-looking, dynamic Christian leaders with all kinds of charisma shouldn't cause you to settle for less than God's standards. Continue to be one of the seven thousand with unbending knees and an undefiled mouth.

Another dangerous tendency of believers in the "7000 club" is to look too much at the Elijahs. Sometimes that is no problem, but present-day Elijahs have running-from-Jezebel times as well as Mount Carmel times. If you keep your eyes on the Elijahs instead of on the Lord, you will be disappointed again and again. Just about the time you become convinced that a certain pastor or Christian leader is the perfect spokesman for God, you hear something about his life that reminds you of Elijah running from Jezebel. What a disappointment and discouragement!

There is also a message here for those of us who find ourselves at times in Elijah-type roles. Think of how greatly encouraged and bolstered in their faith the seven thousand must have been as a result of Elijah's courageous stand at Mount Carmel. Just maybe some of those secret seven thousand believers would have come out of the woodwork if Elijah had not run away so suddenly. What an awesome responsibility we have! The seven thousand are watching us! We never know how many secret believers are encouraged and helped along the way by our outspoken testimony on the one hand, and how many of them are stumbled and hindered and turned off by our "throwing in the towel" on the other hand.

The Scriptures do not give us any more information about most of the seven thousand. However, we do have a few more details about some of them. There was Obadiah—not, by the way, the prophet who wrote a book of the Old Testament—and the one hundred prophets he hid from Jezebel (1 Kings 18:3-16). There was Elisha, who was being prepared to take Elijah's place (1 Kings 19:19-21). There were the prophets of God mentioned in 1 Kings 20:13, 28, and 35. There was Naboth, who refused to let his family inheritance pass into the hands of King Ahab, because God's law was against such transactions (1 Kings 21). And certainly the prophet Micaiah would be counted among the seven thousand (1 Kings 22). Some of those seven thousand were less secret and more outspoken than others. In fact, Micaiah became as fearless before Ahab as Elijah had been. Some of those seven thousand may have had significant shortcomings. Obadiah, for example, was involved in King Ahab's business when maybe he should have separated himself more from the worldly affairs of the royal court. But regardless of their wide differences in courage and commitment, they had one thing in common: the seven thousand had not bowed the knee to Baal nor kissed his image. Every growing Christian today should at least be one of the seven thousand. Can God count on you?

19

Broken Before Blessed

Genesis 32:30-31 So Jacob named the place Peniel, for he said, "I have seen God face to face, yet my life has been preserved." Now the sun rose upon him just as he crossed over Penuel, and he was limping on his thigh.

Read also Genesis 32:24-31.

Many of you have read the story of Joni Eareckson. Joni had a lot of things going for her. She was a good-looking, popular, athletic, and very active teenager. She was also a Christian. What more could she ask for?! But Joni's life was far from what God intended it to be. She says in her book that her teenage life revolved around her own ego and desires. Upon graduation from high school, Joni knew that things were not the greatest between herself and the Lord, and she prayed that somehow God would do something to turn her life around so that she could be used for His glory.

God answered Joni's prayer in a most unusual way. He permitted her to break her neck in a diving accident and to permanently lose the use of her arms and her legs. How could God allow such a tragedy? Joni struggled tremendously with that question for the first few months following her injury. Then she gradually began to realize that God really wanted to draw her closer to Himself and bless her life through that traumatic experience. In reality, God was breaking the old Joni down so that the new Joni in Christ could become a blessing to others. Today Joni's beautiful relationship with God radiates out from her wheelchair to literally thousands of people. Completely fulfilled in Christ, Joni says she would not want it any other way. On each of the pictures she sketches (Joni draws with unbelievable skill by holding a felt tip pen in her mouth!) she writes "Joni PTL." Her "*Praise The Lord*" signature is a constant testimony that blessing can come from brokenness.

"Broken before blessed" is a scriptural principle, and God uses different breaking methods in each of our lives. God's methods are not just physical; they vary, depending on the particular hang-ups and blind spots of each growing Christian. The sudden loss of a scholarship or the unexpected challenge of undesirable responsibilities may be part of the breaking process. The "broken before blessed" principle is very dramatically taught in Genesis 32:24-31 from an event in the life of Jacob.

Jacob was the son of Isaac and the grandson of the great patriarch Abraham. As Jacob grew up, he believed in the God of his fathers, but he was certainly not what we would call totally committed. In fact, the picture we get of Jacob from Scripture is that of a young man who was selfish and all out for "number one." Even when he was a teenager he cheated his brother Esau out of the birthright—certain family rights and privileges that Esau would inherit—(see Genesis 24:27-34). Then some years later he tricked his aging father in order to get the paternal blessing, which also rightfully belonged to the firstborn twin, Esau (see Genesis 27). At that point, Esau was so furious that he determined to kill Jacob as soon as their father Isaac died. Since Jacob had no chance against

Esau in a fight (see Genesis 25:27), he left home. Cheating, cunning, conniving Jacob was on the run! But God was not done with this runaway. Jacob had a lot of lessons to learn, but he would eventually become the man of faith God intended him to be (see Hebrews 11:21). God never gives up on any of His children. You can be sure that, in spite of our selfish and "me-first" ways, the Lord is at work behind the scenes. He is steadily chipping away at our proud and stony hearts. He wants to break us down and open us up for blessing (see Psalm 51:17 and Philippians 1:6).

Jacob put several hundred miles between himself and Esau. He went to the land of his mother's relatives and settled there for twenty years. There he married and began a large family. (His sons were later to become the heads of the twelve tribes of Israel.) During those twenty long years, God taught Jacob and disciplined him. It was certainly not by chance that Jacob had to learn to respect the rights of the firstborn by being forced to marry Leah (see Genesis 29). It wasn't by chance that Jacob's father-in-law, Laban, happened to be as cunning and selfish as Jacob himself! Time and time again they locked horns and tried to selfishly outwit each other (Genesis 28-31). But God used all those circumstances to break Jacob down and prepare him for blessing. How often the Lord will bring us into contact with people and circumstances that rub us the wrong way! That is one of the methods God uses to knock off our rough edges. You don't smooth a rough plank by rubbing it with cotton—you must use an abrasive!

In Genesis 32 we see Jacob finally going home. On the way, he received word that Esau was planning to meet him with four hundred men. Jacob was scared and prayed for his life! He divided his party in two for safety and then sent most of them ahead with gifts to appease Esau. He even put his family in front of him as part of the buffer between himself and his brother. Maybe the still-crafty Jacob planned to run and save his own skin if he saw that Esau would not accept the gifts or show mercy to his family.

While Jacob waited *alone* that night, a man came into his campsite and began to wrestle with him. What was said or how the fight began we don't know, but we do know that Jacob's opponent was no ordinary man. Hosea 12:4 indicates that the stranger was an angel of God. In fact, verse 30 of Genesis 32 intimates that the heavenly visitor may have been *the* angel of the Lord, the prein-carnate Son of God temporarily taking on the appearance of a man (see also Genesis 18). *God* wrestled with Jacob! Jacob had learned a lot of lessons already but, like all of us, he still had a long way to go. Until Jacob was thoroughly broken of his selfishness and scheming, he could not go further in his relationship with God. And so God met Jacob *alone* and wrestled with him one-on-one.

What a picture lesson for us! Is God wrestling with you right now because of some area in your life that needs to be broken down? What about submission to authority—like your folks? What about priorities—like Scripture versus sleep?! What about God's will for your life—like next summer or next year?

The wrestling match was not over in a few minutes; it went on all night. God could easily overpower us, but He does not "zap" us or violate our wills. He patiently wrestles with us to break us down. Near dawn, the Lord put a move on Jacob that evidently caused a slight dislocation of the ball-and-socket joint in Jacob's thigh. It wasn't an illegal hold or a karate chop—just the touch of God in a critical area. Has the Lord touched you in that way yet? The touch of God may be painful at first, but it is part of the breaking process that paradoxically leads to greater blessing in your life as a Christian.

Jacob now was no longer able to wrestle; he could only

cling to God. At last he realized his helplessness and weakness and dependence. Now he wouldn't even be able to run from Esau. His only hope was to hold on and ask for a blessing from the Lord. What a turnaround in the life of Jacob! Each one of us must come to that point. Sometimes it is the area of our greatest natural strength or ability that God must touch in order to cause us to depend on Him. The Lord says, "My grace is sufficient for you, for power is perfected in weakness" (2 Corinthians 12:9).

The next thing we read (Genesis 32:27) is that the Lord asked Jacob his name. Why? Before Jacob could be blessed he had to own up to the reality of what he really was: "the supplanter." That is the meaning of the name *Jacob,* and how well it characterized his life of deceiving and scheming to get what he wanted from others. By giving his name, Jacob openly confessed his wrongdoing. Confession of our sin is part of the breaking process. Before God can fill our lives with His blessings, we must own up to our past failures. It is humbling but necessary.

The stigma of the old name was removed, and Jacob was given a new name, Israel. There is some question as to the exact meaning of the new name, but from the context of Genesis 32:28 and Hosea 12:3-4, it seems that the idea is "he who strives or perseveres with God." Quite a change from "supplanter" to "one who perseveres with God." Notice that verse 28 adds that Jacob prevailed with God. That, of course, does not mean that Jacob won the wrestling match but that he realized his defeat and clung to the only source of hope. The breaking process worked a miracle in the life of Jacob, as it still does in the lives of believers today.

Jacob tried to get the stranger to reveal Himself by giving His name, but was unsuccessful. Jacob still had quite a way to go before the Lord would intimately disclose Himself to Jacob as He had done with Jacob's faithful grandfather, Abraham. (See Genesis 35:1-15 for this stage in Jacob's life as a believer.) But for now the breaking process brought blessing (Genesis 32:29) and the realization that God Himself had touched his life (v. 30).

The view we have of Jacob in verse 31 is a beautiful spiritual picture of the growing Christian who has undergone the breaking process and "prevailed." The sun is shining on one who has wrestled all night. He is making forward progress with a permanent limp. Here is a believer who is broken, but blessed.

20

Kidnapped Through Philosophy

Colossians 2:8 See to it that no one takes you captive through philosophy and empty deception, according to the tradition of men, according to the elementary principles of the world, rather than according to Christ.

Read Colossians 2:3-10.

Whoever heard of being kidnapped through philosophy? I've heard of people being brainwashed or programmed to swallow the doctrines of revolutionary movements, but never through the free study of philosophy! Why, philosophy is the love and pursuit of wisdom and knowledge. How could the pursuit of wisdom ever result in a kidnapping?

The Bible says that it *is* possible to be kidnapped through philosophy. The word "captive" in Colossians 2:8 could be translated "kidnapped." The word means to rob and carry off as booty or as prey or prisoner—like kidnapping. Thus the Bible indicates that it is possible for someone to be carried away from the truth into the slavery of error through philosophy. The Colossian Christians were strongly warned to guard against such a possibility; the same warning is for all growing Christians.

We are told to be careful that not only no one *deludes* us with persuasive arguments (v. 4), but also that no one actually *kidnaps* us through philosophy.

Now the Bible is not knocking philosophy as such in this portion of Scripture. Nor is it condemning all philosophical studies. It is not saying, for example, that a Christian student should not sign up for a course in philosophy. What the Bible is saying, however, is that all philosophy that is not Christ-centered is "hollow and deceptive." Therefore a Christian student should be continually on guard when he does study philosophy, because it is usually written or taught from a non-Christian perspective—precisely where the danger lies.

Many unsuspecting students and others have been deluded and kidnapped by hollow and deceptive philosophies. Deceptive philosophies are not just the false teachings of the "Moonies" and other cults and extremist groups. Those are usually easy to detect—even by the average non-Christian. But deceptive philosophy can be taught right in the classroom by respectable and scholarly men and women. It can sound logical, enlightening, and intellectual. Under such conditions, the Christian student is tempted (as well as peer-pressured) to doubt and conform. His thought patterns may be something like the following: *Maybe my Christian friends are wrong after all. They mean well, but they're naive. Surely my brilliant professors can't be all wrong. Since when does a Christian have a corner on the truth, anyway?* Wait! Let's go back and think this through again before we dismiss all Christians as uninformed people who have committed intellectual suicide.

It was mentioned above that the danger connected with philosophical study lies in the perspective or standpoint from which things are viewed. You see, a person's philosophy is based on the set of presuppositions he has concerning the universe—his world view. Those presuppositions constitute something like a grid in the person's mind, through which all observed and experienced data is received—and interpreted! Thus a person's philosophy (how he puts it all together) is totally dependent on his basic set or "grid" of presuppositions.

The Christian world view is one of many differing basic sets of presuppositions concerning the universe in which we live. The Christian world view is the only world view that is Christ-centered. The Christian world view is what is taught in the Bible. Thus the true Christian believes that, even though his is a minority world view (the majority of people, even in "Christian" lands, do not accept the Christian world view), it is the only completely true one, because it comes from the mind of God.

Perhaps an illustration would be helpful. Consider a large jigsaw puzzle in which every piece of the puzzle represents a piece of truth. Like interlocking jigsaw puzzle pieces, all truth interlocks. There is no piece of truth that is independent of all the rest of the truth. Whether it's truth in the area of mathematics or medicine or morals or whatever makes no difference; it must all hang together. Normally in doing a jigsaw puzzle, we finish the frame first and then we properly fit into that framework all the other areas of the puzzle. The same is true of our philosophy. The framework is our world view or set of presuppositions. All the bits and pieces and sections of truth that we accumulate are fitted and oriented with respect to that framework. If our framework is distorted or put together wrongly, then the other sections will not fit, unless we "force" them in. That is known to puzzle people as "piece-pounding!"

A lot of "piece-pounding" goes on in the area of philosophy. A brilliant non-Christian mathematics professor, for example, may have it all together in his or her area of the puzzle (in fact, far more together than Joe

Average Christian could ever hope to have it together in that area!). *But* Dr. Mathematics now "wedges" his area of specialty along with his other observed data and experience into his own framework of presuppositions. The resulting philosophy may appear to fit together—especially to the student who knows that the professor is a respected authority in his field. However, somewhere along the line that philosophy has some "forced pieces" or weak links of interstices (holes) or loose ends, so that it really doesn't all hang together. In the last analysis, it does not have a solid base—it is hollow! But it looks and sounds good—it is deceptive!

A Christian student may not have the IQ or brains of the non-Christian professor. In terms of the illustration, the Christian student may not be very good at all in doing "jigsaw puzzles," *but* he has the right frame! His set of presuppositions comes from the Bible, and not from his own ideas, which could be biased. As he picks up pieces of truth (some of which he may not understand very well), he can at least put them into the right Christian world view. He doesn't have to piece-pound or distort or fudge or be intellectually dishonest. And the Christian world view really does hang together. It does not leave loose ends dangling, or avoid the tough questions like evil and cruelty and suffering.

Check out some of the other world views and see how those questions are left up in the air. How do the world views of naturalism and existentialism answer those questions, for example? The Christian world view gives answers for such things as miracles and occult phenomena, guilt, love, beauty, and everything else that a world view must account for if it is going to hang together. Do other philosophies give satisfactory answers in those areas?

Colossians 2:8 tells us why philosophy that is not Christ-centered is hollow and deceptive. It is formed "according to the tradition of men, according to the elementary principles of the world, rather than according to Christ." Philosophy that is based on human tradition is man-made—and who is to say *which* man is right? The first basic presupposition of the Christian world view is that the truth originated in the *mind* of God and then was communicated to man by the *mouth* of God. Growing Christians must be particularly cautious about taking ideas that originate in man-made world views and mixing them into the Christian world view.

Consider the theory of evolution, for example. This theory comes out of the world view of naturalism, which holds as a basic presupposition that there is no supernatural. We are but complex machines that have evolved from mere matter through time and chance. Evolution comes out of the world view of naturalism quite naturally! But evolution does *not* come out of the Christian world view naturally. It must be mixed *in* through the concept of theistic evolution. Is theistic evolution biblical, or is it merely an intrusion of a foreign idea into the Christian world view? Take a good hard look at the evidence before you risk being taken in by a philosophy that may indeed have its roots in human tradition rather than Scripture.

Philosophy that is not Christ-centered is hollow and deceptive, not only because it is man-made but also because it depends on "the basic principles of the world." What does that mean? There are several possible interpretations for this phrase, but it seems that the overall idea is that world views that are not Christ-centered are *too small*. They may be adequate and true in some areas, but they are not large enough to account for all of the data of the universe, and they are not large enough to give an adequate basis for what is included in them. The world view of secular humanism, for example, is not large enough to explain or give an adequate philosophical basis for the fact that man is moral.

If Jesus Christ is God, as Colossians 2:9 emphatically states, then He is the center and focus of this universe. "For from Him and through Him and to Him are all things" (Romans 11:36). Any philosophy is bound to be hollow and deceptive, if it is not centered on Christ, "in whom are hidden all the treasures of wisdom and knowledge" (Colossians 2:3). Don't be shortchanged or kidnapped by empty philosophy.

SPRING

21

A Psalm For All Seasons

Psalm 22:1 My God, my God, why hast Thou forsaken Me?
Read all of Psalm 22.

Psalm 22 could be called a Good Friday psalm, because it speaks of the death of the Messiah. It could also be called an Easter psalm, because it speaks of the resurrection of the Messiah. But the death and resurrection of Jesus Christ are events to be remembered not only on Good Friday and Easter Sunday. They are the foundation of the Christian faith. Therefore Psalm 22 could rightly be called a psalm for all seasons. Whenever we Christians read this magnificent psalm, it should cause us to worship our Lord and Savior.

Psalms that are Christ-centered, such as Psalm 22, are known as messianic psalms. Although these psalms were written centuries before Christ, they give us a wealth of truth concerning our Lord Jesus. In most of the messianic psalms the psalmist writes about something from his own experience, but under the inspiration of the Holy Spirit the description goes beyond the experience of the writer and prophetically speaks of Christ.

Psalm 22 is a truly amazing and remarkable messianic

psalm. First of all, it is amazing in its *penetration of the
sufferings* of our Lord. In this psalm we glimpse the
depths of the extreme spiritual sufferings of the Son of
God. Here we are given the awesome privilege of explor-
ing "holy ground" that is largely hidden in the gospel
accounts of the crucifixion. The sufferings of Christ on
the cross were not just the intense physical agonies that
He endured. As the sacrifice for our sins, He also experienced the wrath of God. No martyr of the faith has ever
had to cry out, "My God, my God, why hast Thou
forsaken me?" (v. 1 and Matthew 27:46). And yet that was
our Lord's experience as He was dying on the cross
through hours of blazing sun and chilling darkness (v. 2
and Matthew 27:45).

The answer to the question "Why?" comes in verse 3.
God, who is holy and cannot look upon sin (Habakkuk
1:13), had to turn His back on His only beloved Son, as
Jesus became our substitute—bearing the penalty of our
sins. "He made Him who knew no sin to be sin on our
behalf, that we might become the righteousness of God in
Him" (2 Corinthians 5:21). Think of the commitment of
the Lord Jesus to His Father's will throughout that
ordeal. Even though there was no answer of deliverance
to His cry, He did not turn back or shrink from the final
hour to which the Father had led Him. No Old Testament
believer ever had to experience such silent heavens (Psalm
22:4-5). In the face of such desperate circumstances, His
response to the Father was one of unwavering faith in the
righteous government of God. "Yet Thou art holy, O
Thou who art enthroned upon the praises of Israel" (v.
3). What a contrast to our usual response when difficult
circumstances come. We, of course, are never separated
from our heavenly Father as Jesus was forsaken. But
how much praise for God's righteous ways comes from
our lips when we're in the depths of suffering, with no
deliverance in sight?

In verses 6-8 we see some further experiences on the cross that contributed to our Lord's spiritual sorrow and anguish. He was downtrodden and defenseless like a worm, discredited and despised by the very people He came to save (v. 6). He was mocked and taunted for His faith in the One who had obviously forsaken Him (v. 8 and Mark 15:29-32). And yet His commitment to the Father and His confidence in the Father's sovereign will was in no way weakened from what it had been throughout His life—even from birth (vv. 9-10). Again what a contrast to our weak faith! How often our faith wavers, even when there is very little pressure on us—let alone intense suffering. Perhaps Psalm 22 will cause us not only to bend our knees in more worship but to straighten our backs and square our shoulders in resolute faith, regardless of the pressure.

As a messianic psalm, Psalm 22 is also remarkable in its *prediction of the sufferings* of the Lord Jesus. Even the most ardent skeptic of the Bible must admit that the psalms were written long before the birth of Christ. Copies of the psalms were found among the now-famous Dead Sea Scrolls and were dated at least a hundred years before Christ. Besides the general predictions of our Lord's sufferings on the cross, which we saw in verses 6-8, and which continue in verses 11-13, there are some specific prophecies concerning His crucifixion in verses 14-18. The critic will try to evade the so-called "vague" or general predictions by saying that they were just experiences of the psalmist, David. The bulls and lion of verses 12-13, for example, are not the heartless mob that jeered our dying Lord, but merely the enemies of King David. The critic will even say that Jesus artificially made verse 1 into a "prophecy" by quoting it from the cross. However, the vivid and detailed language of crucifixion in verses 14-18 is hard for any skeptic to get around.

Although Psalm 22 may have its roots in some trying

experience of David, it certainly transcends that experience completely in verses 14-18. When were all of David's
bones out of joint, for example (v. 14)? Yet that is exactly
what happened to a body suspended in crucifixion as the
cross was mercilessly dropped into the earthen hole. And
when were David's hands and feet pierced (v. 16)? For that
matter, how often was piercing practiced in crucifixion?
The normal method was to tie the hands and feet to the
cross. The prophetic evidence for the crucifixion of Christ
from this contested verse (v. 16) is overwhelming. Profuse
perspiration (v. 14), heart prostration (v. 14), physical
exhaustion (v. 15), extreme thirst (v. 15), partial nudity
(vv. 17-18), and hurt to modesty (v. 17) are further descrip-
tions that add to the graphic picture of crucifixion and
should be read in conjunction with the gospel accounts
of our Lord's death (see Matthew 27, Mark 15, Luke 23,
and John 19). And remember that crucifixion was not a
form of execution common to the time and culture of
David. It was a Roman method, and therefore came into
use long after Psalm 22 was written.

In addition to describing the sufferings of the crucifixion, Psalm 22 also details the activity of the soldiers
who were there (v. 18). Roman soldiers considered the
clothes of the victim as spoils of the execution. They
would generally divide or tear apart a poor peasant's
clothing to use as rags for cleaning weapons, etc. According to John 19:23, that is exactly what they did to Christ's
outer garments. However, in accordance with the prophetic detail of casting lots (Psalm 22:18), we note in
John 19:24 that the soldiers gambled for Jesus' seamless
tunic. All of those details of the crucifixion of Christ were
carried out by individuals who had no idea of the predictions of Psalm 22. Do you want proof of the inspiration
of the Bible? What better proof could you ask for?

The *perspective of the sufferings* of Christ presented in
Psalm 22 is also important to observe and appreciate.

Notice that the Messiah Himself is the speaker through-out most of the psalm. In verses 1-21 He is speaking from the perspective of suffering on the cross. But verses 22-31 are spoken from the perspective of victory after the resurrection. Our Lord's death comes between verses 21 and 22. That is why the spear-thrust of the Roman soldier, which occurred after the Lord died (John 19:33-34), is not included in the psalm. We know from the New Testament that the wrath of God against our sin was fully satisfied before Christ died, because He proclaimed in triumph, "It is finished!" (John 19:30). We can appreciate that truth from verse 21 of the psalm, because the Lord was answered (not just heard) by the Father before He died. His time of being forsaken by God was over. Our Lord commended His human spirit into the Father's care, and then physically died (Luke 23:46).

Now notice the joy of resurrection beginning in verse 22. The Savior is no longer alone. He is declaring the Father's name in the midst of His *brethren* (Psalm 22:22). That includes us! (see Hebrews 2:11-12). What a position we have been given as a result of Christ's atoning work on the cross! In verses 26-31, our attention is drawn to the results of our Lord's death and resurrection. The scope of those verses is not limited to the present time; they certainly look forward to Christ's second coming. The poor and afflicted will be relieved (v. 26). The whole earth will recognize the lordship of Christ (vv. 27-29). The righteousness of Christ and His *finished* work ("per-formed" in verse 31) will be declared to generation after generation throughout the rest of man's history on earth (vv. 30-31). The theme of Psalm 22 is not only appropriate for all seasons—it is the theme of all history! It is only a matter of time before the entire universe recognizes the truth of Psalm 22.

22

If Christ Had Not Risen

1 Corinthians 15:12-20 Now if Christ is preached, that He has been raised from the dead, how do some among you say that there is no resurrection of the dead? But if there is no resurrection of the dead, not even Christ has been raised; and if Christ has not been raised, then our preaching is vain, your faith also is vain. Moreover we are even found to be false witnesses of God, because we witnessed against God that He raised Christ, whom He did not raise, if in fact the dead are not raised. For if the dead are not raised, not even Christ has been raised; and if Christ has not been raised, your faith is worthless; you are still in your sins. Then those also who have fallen asleep in Christ have perished. If we have hoped in Christ in this life only, we are of all men most to be pitied. But now Christ has been raised from the dead, the first fruits of those who are asleep.

Easter is a unique feature of Christianity. That is no because more "Christians" go to church on that Sunday but because Easter celebrates the resurrection of Jesu Christ from the dead. Christianity teaches that its founde is living today! No other religion of the world make such a startling claim. Other religions may claim that the "spirit" of their founder lives on today in his religious teachings, but Christianity claims that Jesus Himself lives today—bodily! Biblical Christianity teaches that Jesus Christ really died but then arose physically (not just spiritually) from the grave and presented Himself alive to many different people on many different occasions over a period of forty days (see Acts 1:3 and 1 Corinthians 15:3-8). Christianity further teaches that after those undeniable physical appearances, Jesus Christ bodily left this earth and promised to return physically someday (John 14:1-3 and Acts 1:9-11). Although we Christians know and experience the *spiritual* presence of our living Lord Jesus now, we look forward to His *physical* return. True Christian faith holds that Jesus Christ was resurrected from the dead bodily, ascended into heaven bodily, lives today in glory bodily, and will someday return to this earth bodily.

The physical resurrection of Jesus Christ from the dead is the keystone of the Christian faith. Christianity stands or falls at that point. In other words, Christianity is ultimately based not only on ethical and religious teachings (as in other world religions) but on a historical event! The foundation of our faith is not just what Jesus *taught* but what He *did* in history to back up His claims. You see, any self-styled religious leader can proclaim certain ethical and virtuous and noble teachings; he may even dare to say, "I am the good shepherd." Some would even go further and say, "I lay down my life for my sheep" and then actually die for "some good cause." But who can continue those statements as Jesus did (John 10:14-18) and claim a physical resurrection? ". . . I lay down My life that I may take it again. No one has taken it away from Me, but I lay it down on My own initiative. I have authority to lay it down, and I have authority to take it up again" (vv. 17-18). What a claim! The ethical teachings of Jesus are inseparable from His claims about

Himself and His power over death. If Jesus Christ did not bodily rise from the dead, then He was a deceiver (not even a good man), and Christianity is a fraud and a farce; Christians are just playing around at religious games.

Scripture teaches that such radical statements are logical conclusions, if indeed the resurrection of Christ did not take place. In 1 Corinthians 15:12-19 we are given several conclusions to which we *must* come if Christ has not risen from the dead. Without the bodily resurrection of Christ, Christianity is stripped of its basis and power.

The apostle Paul wrote this passage to the Corinthian believers who were confused over the concept of the future physical resurrection of Christians who had already died. They did not doubt the resurrection of Christ; they believed in it wholeheartedly (v. 11). But the concept of a bodily resurrection for believers was hard for them to grasp. Apparently they did not have any problem with the idea of the spirit's living on in some other world, because the immortality of the soul was certainly part of the prevalent Greek philosophy. But the resurrection of the body was a new revelation for them—a mind-blower!

The apostle directed the attention of the Corinthian believers to the Lord's resurrection. If they believed in the physical resurrection of Christ, why should they find the concept of the physical resurrection of the Christian so hard to grasp (v. 12)? If God raised Jesus Christ from human death, it was logical that He could raise any person from the dead. But the opposite was logically true too! If there was no such thing as the physical resurrection of persons from the dead, then even Christ could not have been raised (vv. 13, 16). After all, Jesus (although He was God) was a real flesh-and-blood person, and He really died. Where does that logic lead us, then? If Christ was not raised, the Christian faith has no solid foundation, and everything about it is "up for grabs."

That logical conclusion is as true today as it was in

Paul's day. If Christ is not risen, our preaching is empty (v. 14). The nice-sounding words contain no reality. What authority do we have for even preaching "love your neighbor as yourself" (Leviticus 19:18)— let alone the resurrection—if Christ is still dead? We become humanistic preachers with no higher authority than what the majority of the people "feel" is right—a totally subjective and relative consensus! If Jesus is not living today, the message of the Bible is void of authority and hollow—our preaching is empty!

If Christ is not risen, our faith is empty (1 Corinthians 15:14). There is no foundation for our Christian faith, if Easter is a hoax. Pinning our destiny on the teachings and claims of a man who is dead is just wishful thinking. What guarantee do we have that there is any hope beyond the cemetery, if the One who claimed that He could conquer death is, in reality, dead Himself? Christian faith based on the teachings of a dead Christ is like a beautiful castle built on thin air.

If Christ is not risen, we are false witnesses of God (v. 15). We are not just deluded religious fanatics playing church—we are downright liars! Of course if God does not really exist, then it doesn't matter much if we're liars, since there are no absolute standards. However, if God does exist but did not raise Christ from the dead, and yet we go on celebrating Easter, then we have distorted the truth and become false witnesses against God Himself (v. 15). That is what we *must* conclude, if there is no physical resurrection from the dead (v. 16).

If Christ is not risen, our faith is worthless; we are still in our sins (v. 17). Not only is our faith without foundation (v. 14), but it is useless. What good is it? Does it give us salvation? No way! Not if the One who claimed He would take away our sins is still in a tomb near Jerusalem. If some kind of payment for the wrongs is not made, there can be no forgiving or forgetting of sins in a moral

universe. If the One in whom we placed our faith as
Savior never triumphed over death, what proof do we
have that any debt has been paid? Without the resurrection, the death penalty for our sins remains (Romans
6:23). We are still held liable for our wrongdoings. We are
still in our sins—*guilty!* If there is no resurrection, there
is no redemption and no reconciliation with God.

If Christ is not risen, those "who have fallen asleep in
Christ have perished" (v. 18). If Easter is a sham, then
Christians who have died are forever lost. There will be
no awakening from the grave. The familiar Christian
epitaph, "Asleep in Jesus," is just a euphemism for
"condemned to death forever." The word "perished"
does not mean annihilation or extinction but rather loss
and ruin. It is loss, not of being, but of well-being. Any
so-called "light at the end of a dark tunnel" (which
supposedly certain "clinically dead" persons have talked
about) is not necessarily the "light of heaven," as many
people would like to assume (see Hebrews 9:17).

If Christ is not risen, and if we have hope in Christ
only for this life, we are to be pitied more than all men
(1 Corinthians 15:19). Why? Because we have sacrificed
and surrendered and suffered and labored and hoped for
nothing but an illusion. If Jesus is not alive today, we are
superstitious fools living in a dream world. This fantasy
may give us peace of mind and hope in this life, but so
what? Why all the sweat and tears if it's all a delusion? As
far as the apostle Paul is concerned, if there is no resurrection, we ought to "live it up" and "do our own thing."
That is exactly what he says in verse 32. Without Easter,
dead Christians have perished (v. 18), and living Christians are to be pitied (v. 19).

But Christ *has* been raised from the dead (v. 20)! What a
glorious relief! All those previous deductions are swept
away with this one great truth. The resurrection of the
Lord Jesus Christ is the proof and power of Christianity.

The empty tomb guarantees the Christian's hope. As the early fruit is the promise of the harvest soon to come, so the resurrection of our Lord is the guarantee that death has been conquered for every Christian. Hallelujah!

23

Criticism: Constructive or Constrictive?

Numbers 12:1-2 Then Miriam and Aaron spoke against Moses because of the Cushite woman whom he had married (for he had married a Cushite woman); and they said, "Has the Lord indeed spoken only through Moses? Has He not spoken through us as well?" And the Lord heard it.
Read Numbers 12.

Criticism of others is a sin! It is a sin that we find easy to excuse in ourselves; we label it "constructive criticism." But our so-called "constructive criticism" is very often "constrictive criticism." Rather than encouraging and helping our friends, we stifle their personalities and stunt their growth as persons by our "constrictive" comments. Negative comments can be destructive and damaging in the lives of other people. And we who engage in the deadly practice of habitually criticizing others are guilty of a deep-rooted sin, the sin of pride. For that reason, the Bible teaches that criticism of others is very wrong, and leads to serious consequences.

In Numbers 12 we read of Moses' being criticized by his brother, Aaron, and his sister, Miriam. Miriam and Aaron found fault with Moses on two grounds: his marriage (v.

1) and his ministry (v. 2). Moses had married a woman of another race, and Miriam and Aaron did not approve of his choice of a wife. We don't know exactly whether the Cushite woman was from Africa or Asia. (The King James translation of "Ethiopia" is possibly misleading at this point.) Furthermore, we don't know whether the Cushite woman was the Zipporah from Midian whom Moses had married earlier (Exodus 2:16-21), or a second wife that Moses had married after the death of Zipporah. But in any case, Miriam and Aaron had no basis for their criticism of Moses' choice.

Miriam and Aaron also criticized Moses because of his position as God's leading spokesman. Miriam and Aaron were jealous of Moses, because they felt he had an unfair monopoly on revelations from the Lord. Remember that both Miriam and Aaron had been given important roles to play in the covenant community. God made Miriam a prophetess (Exodus 15:20) and Aaron the high priest. Although they had significant positions, they were still jealous of Moses and his "higher" position.

Miriam's and Aaron's complaints about Moses' marriage and ministry were typical of all personal criticism. We either criticize the *person* himself or something about his *position*. Derogatory comments about someone else's looks or mannerisms or abilities or choices are critical of that person as an individual. How often we make fun of a person's large nose, eating habits, athletic inabilities, or choice of clothes. Are we any better than Miriam and Aaron, who criticized Moses' choice of a mate? Sometimes our poisonous comments have to do with another's achievements or responsibilities or authority. That kind of remark is basically critical of the person's position. Are any of us innocent of belittling a fellow student's efforts in student government or as an R.A., of pointing out our boss's "inadequacies," or knocking our spiritual leaders for their way of getting things done? Is that any different

from the conduct of Miriam and Aaron when they criticized the leadership ministry of Moses?

Why were Miriam and Aaron critical of Moses? The
basic problem was pride. Remember that Aaron was the
older brother of Moses. During the confrontation with
Pharoah in Egypt, Aaron had a more up-front role as the
spokesman for Moses. Now, however, older brother Aaron
had been put in what he probably considered a backseat
position. Aaron's hurt ego manifested itself in unfavorable remarks. Miriam's role as prophetess probably gave
rise to a desire to be more in the limelight. If God was
speaking to the people through her prophecies, why
shouldn't she have more of a leadership role? Most likely
Miriam's pride was further pricked when the ability to
prophesy was also given to seventy elders (Numbers 11:24-
30). And maybe there was even some jealousy between
Miriam and Moses' wife as to who was the "First Lady of
the Camp"! In any case, Miriam's proud spirit was hurt,
and the result was criticism of Moses.

When our pride is pricked, it isn't long before we're
guilty of the same. Criticism of others is like the leaves of
the tree of pride. Think of the roots and trunk of that tree
as the basic sin of pride. Now when the sin of pride is not
being controlled in our lives, it branches out into all
kinds of other evils. Some of the branches of the tree of
pride are jealousy, contempt, refusal to submit to authority, ego trips, and arrogance. Those branches (and many
others) are always behind the leaves of criticism. When a
leaf of personal criticism is displayed, it is certain that the
root of pride is in our hearts.

The seriousness of the sin becomes shockingly clear
when we observe the Lord's reaction to the words of
Miriam and Aaron. The Lord not only heard their remarks (a fact we tend to overlook when we criticize
others!), but He disciplined Miriam and Aaron for their
sin. "The anger of the LORD *burned* against them" (Num-

bers 12:9). That leaves no doubt that the Lord does not take a lenient, "everybody does it" view of criticism. The fact that Miriam became a leper further emphasizes the gravity of her sin. You may wonder, "Why didn't Aaron get leprosy too?" The answer is definitely *not* that God has male chauvinist tendencies, as some critics distortedly teach! The answer is contained in the first verse, but it is not detected in our English translations. The verb "spoke" in verse 1 is in the *feminine singular* form in the Hebrew text. That would indicate that Miriam probably initiated and led in the criticism.

The type of discipline God used cut through the leaves and branches to the root problem of pride. It is pretty difficult to be proud as a leper! God's discipline of us will always deal with our basic problems—not just the surface symptoms. We can be sure that we will "eat humble pie" in some way if we "mouth off" in criticism. Is it possible that some recent humbling experience in your life was allowed by God in order to stem the tide of unkind remarks flowing out of your mouth?

The sin of putting down others invariably affects a number of people detrimentally. It's often been said that you can't sin in a vacuum. Notice that the Lord departed (v. 9). Think of it. The presence of the Lord departed from Israel because of *personal criticism!* Is it possible that you are not experiencing much of the living presence of the Lord within your Christian fellowship because of too much criticism of one another—maybe your own negative comments? Notice also that the whole camp of Israel could not move forward until the sin of criticism was judged (vv. 15-16). Is it possible that my criticism of others is hindering the spiritual progress of my brothers and sisters in Christ?

How should we deal with our tendency to criticize others, once we recognize and confess this sin? Just knowing the seriousness should help us put a seal on our lips and be afraid to criticize others (v. 8). Furthermore, we should be like Moses and not retaliate. So often our criticism of others is "return fire." Notice that Moses did not take verbal revenge—even though it would have been easy for him to have done so from his position of authority. He followed the scriptural principle—"never take your own revenge" (Romans 12:19). Like Moses, we should pray for others—even those who criticize us (v. 13). It's amazing how our criticism of another person tapers off as we begin to pray specifically and sincerely for that person.

There is a place for legitimate, helpful, and constructive evaluation in our relationships with other people. However, to be sure that our comments are not *constrictive* criticism, we should follow two scriptural principles. The first is the principle of "private confrontation," found in Matthew 18:15. Let us make our constructive comments directly to the person—not behind his back. And let us do it in private—not in front of others. The second principle is the "log before splinter" principle found in Matthew 7:3-5. Let us make sure that the telephone pole is out of our own eyes *before* we try to remove specks of sawdust from the eyes of others! If we follow those scriptural principles, our comments to others can be truly helpful and constructive, not constrictive.

24

Get the Big Picture

Jonah 4:9-11 Then God said to Jonah, "Do you have good reason to be angry about the plant?" And he said, "I have good reason to be angry, even to death." Then the LORD said, "You had compassion on the plant for which you did not work, and which you did not cause to grow, which came up overnight and perished overnight. And should I not have compassion on Nineveh, the great city in which there are more than 120,000 persons who do not know the difference between their right and left hand, as well as many animals?"

Read all of chapter 4 and, if possible, the whole book of Jonah before proceeding.

The little book of Jonah in the Old Testament is more than just the historical record of a Jewish prophet who was swallowed by a big fish. It is the Word of God. Because it is Scripture, it is packed full of lessons for the growing Christian. As God worked with His servant Jonah many years ago, so He works with His servants today.

In the first three chapters of the book we find that Jonah disobeyed the Lord by running away from a job

that the Lord wanted him to do. Instead of preaching in
the wicked city of Nineveh, as God commanded, Jonah
sailed away toward Tarshish, a city at least 2,500 miles in
the opposite direction. But God, in His disciplining love,
brought Jonah back. We know that the return trip was
quite traumatic for Jonah, but that's usually the way it is.
When God's servants disobey, the return to obedience is
often through discipline.

Jonah was recommissioned (3:1) and preached boldly
in Nineveh, that great capital city of the ancient Assyrian
Empire. The result was one of the greatest revivals in
history. From the king on down, the people of Nineveh
repented of their evil ways (3:5), and God withheld His
judgment (3:10). Nineveh was spared for another 200
years until overthrown by Babylon in 612 B.C. What we
learn of God in the book of Jonah is a far cry from the
misinformed idea that the God of the Old Testament was
a cruel, vindictive God who limited His grace to the
Jewish people. The story of Jonah is just one example of
God's love extended well beyond the borders of Israel to
the pagan nations of the ancient world.

As we come to chapter 4, we are surprised to find Jonah
really upset! Instead of being elated over the results of his
ministry, Jonah was *very* angry (4:1). Why? Because he
didn't really want the mercy of the Lord extended to
Nineveh (4:2). After all, the Assyrians were the archene-
mies of Israel. Jonah would rather have seen his warning
and pronouncement of judgment realized. Let those Assyrians get what's coming to them! They deserve to go to
hell without any mercy!

Is it possible that we feel the same way about some
people whom God loves? What about the thousands who
are in prison in this country—even murderers?

Jonah was so upset with God that he wanted to die
(4:3). Have you ever been so frustrated and angry with the
circumstances in your life that you felt the same way?

God wants us to be mature servants, but many times we act like children—selfish, spoiled, and short-sighted.

Jonah pouted all the way out of the city and set up some kind of makeshift observation post (4:5) in hope that maybe, just maybe, God would still destroy Nineveh—maybe even send fire from heaven.

Because of Jonah's attitude, God had to reprove his servant, and that's what the rest of chapter 4 is all about. In verses 6-8 we see the Lord giving Jonah an object lesson in order to help His servant visualize his own problem and see how selfish his attitude really was. First a shade plant grew up, under which Jonah could sit in comfort while he waited for the "fireworks." Jonah was very pleased with it (4:6). But then the Lord had a worm come along the next day and destroy the very plant that He Himself had given for Jonah's comfort. When the hot eastern sun came up, Jonah was ready to throw in the towel again. He was so depressed that he even begged the Lord "with all his soul" to take his life (4:8).

How easy it is to see ourselves in Jonah. When we are not right with the Lord, our feelings run like a roller coaster. One day we're way up and "extremely happy" (4:6), but the next day we're down in the depths, feeling sorry for ourselves and wishing we were dead (4:8). Such very small things (a little worm) can ruin our whole day—a B+ instead of an A-—a scratch on our car or furniture—an empty mailbox—a small tear in our new sweater—a rainy day! God wants His servants to grow up and get the *big* picture—*His* viewpoint! As in the case of Jonah, the Lord often gives us things that we don't deserve for our own comfort—perhaps He even lets us have something we had our hearts set on. We become very happy and even take that blessing as a sign of God's approval on our lives and actions.

But it may not be a sign of God's approval at all; it may be part of a lesson that God wants to teach us, or maybe just the goodness of God to undeserving servants. Everything we have is only by the goodness of God, anyway. But, like Jonah, how we often get upset if the Lord takes away any of our little comforts! We act like spoiled and selfish children. We can't see that He has a very good reason for doing so, although we may never fully understand it in this lifetime (see Job 1:21). When the Lord takes something from us, let us patiently look for the lesson He may have for us, instead of becoming angry and resentful with God, who has the big picture.

The Lord drove home the point of His object lesson to Jonah (vv. 9-11), and it went something like this: "Jonah, why are you so upset? Can't you see that you're being selfish and short-sighted? You're so concerned about that *one plant,* Jonah, but I'm concerned about *one hundred twenty thousand people.* Don't you see that those people are Mine, Jonah? I made them. I love them. I don't want them to perish! Jonah, you're not even concerned about the many animals that would be destroyed, never mind the people! My dear servant Jonah, I love you, but please grow up and get the big picture."

What a lesson! So often we get hung up on the incidentals, while the world around us is perishing. We're more interested in our room than our roommate; our bonus than our boss; our touchdown than our teammate; our fun than our family. How it must hurt God to see His children so interested in the "toys" He has given them that they are insensitive to the needs of others. Let us grow up and see things from the perspective of our heavenly Father.

Did Jonah learn the lesson? He must have, because he wrote the book! It takes a big man to write about his own obstinacy and immmaturity. In fact, our Lord refers to Jonah as a great prophet (Luke 11:32). Yes, Jonah learned the lesson that God is constantly trying to teach *us:* Grow up and get the big picture.

25

Born Free

Colossians 3:1-10 If then you have been raised up with Christ, keep seeking the things above, where Christ is, seated at the right hand of God. Set your mind on the things above, not on the things that are on earth. For you have died and your life is hidden with Christ in God. When Christ, who is our life, is revealed, then you also will be revealed with Him in glory. Therefore consider the members of your earthly body as dead to immorality, impurity, passion, evil desire, and greed, which amounts to idolatry. For it is on account of these that the wrath of God will come, and in them you also once walked, when you were living in them. But now you also, put them all aside: anger, wrath, malice, slander, and abusive speech from your mouth. Do not lie to one another, since you laid aside the old self with its evil practices, and have put on the new self who is being renewed to a true knowledge according to the image of the One who created him.

Born Free is the heart-warming story of a lion cub named Elsa who was adopted as a family pet. But Elsa was not created to live in captivity. She was born free and was meant to live free. However, when freedom came, it was a real struggle for Elsa to appreciate her new freedom, because she had lived so long in captivity. The young lioness found it extremely difficult to separate from the life she was used to. Finally Elsa was able to break free of the old ties and adapt properly to the environment for which she was created.

Many growing Christians are like Elsa. God has given us a brand new life of freedom in Jesus Christ—we've been born free (see John 8:36; 2 Corinthians 5:17). Now God wants us to live in the light of that freedom. He does not want us to be held captive by any sin. But what a struggle it is to break free from the old habits and hang-ups. At times it seems impossible. But God's Word assures us that victory is possible. Romans 6:14 says, "sin shall not be master over you." We are born free!

The scriptural method of victory over sin is *not* "try with all your might to be good." That's like bending over and trying to pick yourself up off the floor by pulling on your shoelaces. It will never happen! God's way to triumph over sin in your life is outlined in Colossians 3:1-10. It is basically a threefold process involving realization, aspiration, and mortification—let's call it the RAM method for short.

Realization is understanding and appreciating *all* that God has done for us in Jesus Christ. Verses 1-4 indicate that when we became Christians we received much more than "fire insurance" and a "ticket to heaven." When we committed our lives to Jesus Christ as Lord, there was more than forgiveness of sins involved in the transaction. We died with Christ (v. 3); we were raised with Christ (v. 1); we have been given new life in Christ (v. 4); we will be glorified with Christ (v. 4).

Now let's repeat those truths and make them personal. God sees an old me crucified with Christ. God sees a new me resurrected with Christ. The new me is therefore *free* from the penalty and power of sin. God sees every Christian that way! Although each Christian still has physical life, he now has new spiritual life within him, and the source of that life is not earthly. The source and center and focus of the new life is Christ Himself, who is now in heaven—unseen by the world at large (v. 3). Someday Christ is going to be revealed to this world in all His glory. At His return, every Christian will share in that glory—and it will be plain for all to see (v. 4). These are fantastic truths! We cannot "feel" these facts now, but we know them to be true—we *realize* them (Romans 6:11).

Aspiration is setting your mind on things above and not on the things of this earth (v. 2). Now that does not mean that we are to walk around with our heads in the clouds and never think about our earthly responsibilities such as homework, borrowed books, and bills! It means, rather, that the center of our attention, interests, and thoughts should be in the things of God (Philippians 4:8). If our new life is bound up in the Lord Jesus Christ, then our minds should ultimately be set on Him—a Christ mindset! If your mind has Jesus as its focal point, you will not be preoccupied with sin. Think back on some of your closest moments with the Lord. Did you feel like sinning then?

"All right," you say, "those times are beautiful, but they are rare in my life. How come I'm always struggling with sin?" Setting your mind on things above does not happen automatically. Every Christian has within him two tendencies, or natures: a divine nature because of his new spiritual life in Christ and a sinful nature (the flesh) because of the present, temporary condition of his earthly body. Even though every Christian has the Holy Spirit to empower the new life, he will still experience conflict because of the flesh (see Galatians 5:17).

But aspiration leads to victory! It's like owning two cars—an old one and a brand new one. You are *free* to drive the new, but you must take definite action and stop driving the old car. Aspiration makes you drive the new car, or "put on the new self" (Colossians 3:10). Aspiration includes putting gas in the new car; Bible study, prayer, worship, and Christian fellowship are high-test gas! Reading trashy magazines and watching lousy TV shows and movies are not aspiration! If that is how you've been running your life lately, then don't expect victory over sin! Setting our minds on things above will not only keep us from sin but will continually result in a more Christlike life (Ephesians 4:22-24). Another way to describe aspiration is "walking by the Spirit" (Romans 8:4; Galatians 5:16, 25). Like walking, aspiration is not automatic, but it is learned and practiced *step by step*.

Mortification is considering the members of your earthly body as dead to sin (v. 5). Now that in no way implies literal amputation or mutilation of our bodies. It implies, rather, a ruthless rejection of all habits and practices that we know to be wrong (Matthew 5:29-30). Remember, as far as God is concerned, the "old you" has died in Christ. Therefore "lay aside the old self with its evil practices" (Colossians 3:9). In terms of the illustration above, mortification is keeping the old car in the garage. Don't even "test drive" it. Many Christians think they can take the old car out for a little drive every once in a while, but they risk ending up in an accident. Involvement in impure and greedy activities such as premarital sexual excesses or "me first" tactics is like driving the old car (v. 5). Those things are not pleasing to God (v. 6). We used to drive the old car because that's all we had (v. 7), but God has given us a brand new one instead—not just a new paint job on the old model! God has condemned the old car to the "garage of death." Let us leave it where God has placed it! Remember, the old car won't go very far with no gas in it! You say you don't have victory over sin? Where have you been buying gas lately—and for which car?

God does not want us chained or captive to any sin in

this life. We will not be *perfect* until we get to heaven (1 John 1:8), but victory over sin in our lives is possible. We've been born free!

26

One-on-One

John 4:10 Jesus answered and said to her, "If you
knew the gift of God, and who it is who says to you,
'Give Me a drink,' you would have asked Him, and
He would have given you living water."
Read John 4:1-42.

"Personal evangelism is just not my thing—it's not my
gift! As long as I lead a godly life, others will see Christ in
me. That's all I'm supposed to do."

Does that sound familiar? There are so many feeble
excuses for not witnessing for our Lord Jesus, but none is
valid. We have a mandate to verbalize the gospel! We are
falling short of our Lord's Commission (Matthew 28:19)
if we are *just* living godly lives. It's true that some
Christians are gifted in the area of personal evangelism,
and a few find it quite easy to share their faith, but we are
all called to be "ambassadors for Christ" (2 Corinthians
5:20).

Personal evangelism is carried out one-on-one—at "the
gut level." It is personally sharing the faith in such a way
that the gospel of Jesus Christ is clearly presented, and a
personal decision is called for, in one way or another.
That one-on-one evangelism may take place over a period

of weeks, or it may be a one-shot deal—like a two-hour flight or a twenty-minute chairlift ride at a ski area.

In John 4 we have an example of our Lord's doing personal evangelism. Jesus is quite tired, and the noon sun is hot, but He is deeply concerned about a soul in search of "water." The Lord speaks just seven times to the Samaritan woman, but contained in each statement is a principle for personal evangelism. Let us learn and apply those principles.

In the first words of Christ to the woman we have the principle of making contacts and building relationships with nonbelievers. Jesus met with a social outcast and began a relationship on the basis of something very common to them both, water. She was a Samaritan prostitute, and the Lord broke through several cultural barriers by asking her for a drink of water. According to social custom a Jewish teacher was not to speak to a woman in public. But Jesus broke that barrier of tradition and even made Himself dependent upon her to meet His thirst. Then the barrier of prejudice was broken down. Samaritans were only partially Jewish in their heritage, and the Jews considered them half-breeds. Racism was so acute that some Jews would not even walk on Samaritan soil in their travels between Judea and Galilee. They would actually cross the Jordan River and take the long way around Samaria, so as not to "have dealings with Samaritans" (v. 9). But Jesus purposely went directly through Samaria (v. 4), met with this Samaritan woman, and was even willing to drink from the same water jar that she drank from!

What a lesson for us! How can we ever begin to communicate the love of God to those in need, if we refuse to make contact and build relationships with those outside our usual social group? The homosexual down the hall in your dorm is in desperate need of the liberation found only in Christ. What do you have in common with

that soul in bondage? Do you take a course together?
Maybe the only thing common to you both is your daily
need for water! That is where Jesus began with the
Samaritan woman. Let me warn you—you may actually
be put down by "well-meaning" brothers and sisters in
your efforts to build relationships, but then so was our
Lord (v. 27 and Matthew 9:10-11).

Christ's second statement to the woman stresses the
uniqueness of Christianity. It is not just another religion
in which one chalks up good works. We must let the non-
Christian know "the gift of God and who" (v. 10). True
Christianity is a relationship with the living Lord, which
anyone can have for the asking. But how can that friend
or neighbor of yours "ask Him" if he doesn't *know*? May
the "if you knew" statement of our Lord be a challenge to
us. We are beggars who have found bread. Our job is to
let other beggars know where they can find it too.

As the Lord continues the conversation, we see Him
explaining just what Christianity has to offer (vv. 13-14).
Jesus does not offer a high-paying job after graduation or
the answers for your next test, but He does offer new and
everlasting life. It is interesting to see how the Lord used
the original point of contact (physical H_2O) as an object
lesson of the spiritual life that He offers. Every person has
a spiritual "thirst" that can be quenched only by God.
We must communicate to the nonbeliever that the new
life Christ offers is not a temporary physical cure but a
permanent spiritual thirst-quencher.

The woman's interest was aroused to the point where
she wanted what Jesus had to offer, even though she was
still thinking in physical terms (v. 15). At this point *we*
would probably try to "close the deal" with prayer, and
welcome another sister or brother into the family! But
our Lord's next statement shows that she was not ready
yet. "Go call your husband and come back!" means that
the masks must come off! The Samaritan woman had to

own up to her past life, and every one of us must "go" and "come back" before the Lord as we really are.

The woman's moral responsibility before her Creator is further pressed home in the Lord's fifth statement (vv. 17-18). She was confronted with her sin of adultery—"the man you now have is not your husband." A person cannot play games with God, who knows *all*, but must face up to the fact of sin in his life. In personal evangelism we are not to point the finger and condemn others; even so, a nonbeliever *must* come to the point where he is willing to admit that he is a sinner before an infinitely holy God.

The woman was convicted. She perceived that the voice of God had been speaking to her soul (v. 19). Feeling the pressure of moral responsibility, she naturally tried to escape by asking a typical "religious" question (v. 20). For hundreds of years her people had not worshiped in Jerusalem but on their own mountain. Our Lord's response is beautiful. He did not get sidetracked with religious tangents, but stayed with the important issue of her *need*. She needed a true and spiritual relationship with God as her heavenly Father. The questions of the "where's and why's" of worship have their place, but let us remember the real need of the person to whom we are witnessing.

The sixth statement by our Lord is loaded with teaching in reference to the woman's religious question. Jesus did not ignore her question, but neither did He spend a lot of time on elaborate theological arguments; what she really needed was *life* in the family of God. Only then would her worship be true and accepted (vv. 23-24). In personal evangelism there is always the temptation to win an argument or show off our knowledge (the Lord could have gone on for hours at this point!), but our goal is to win the soul.

Finally the Samaritan woman came to the point where

she really wanted Christ. She was through with her questions and arguments. When she admitted that the coming Messiah would have the answers, she admitted that she needed the Lord. And so in the seventh and last statement the Lord revealed Himself: "I who speak to you am He" (v. 26). Every soul who comes to that point of decision and asks for Christ *will* find Him.

The proof of the woman's salvation is found in the next few verses. She leaves her waterpot and begins to do personal evangelism! (The forgotten waterpot could symbolize the things that used to satisfy her deepest desires—how insignificant, compared to a fountain of living water!) The converted prostitute's willingness and courage to share her new faith with those who knew all about her brought amazing results (vv. 39-42). One-on-one evangelism always brings amazing blessing. Try it!

27

Peace and Quiet

1 Timothy 2:1-6 First of all, then, I urge that entreaties and prayers, petitions and thanksgivings, be made on behalf of all men, for kings and all who are in authority, in order that we may lead a tranquil and quiet life in all godliness and dignity. This is good and acceptable in the sight of God our Savior, who desires all men to be saved and to come to the knowledge of the truth. For there is one God, and one mediator also between God and men, the man Christ Jesus, who gave Himself as a ransom for all, the testimony borne at the proper time.

News is coming fast and furious these days! The Middle East is in conflict. Energy crises are constantly threatening to engulf us. And the country's top executives have our heads spinning.

What are concerned Christians to do about such chaotic conditions? Should we repent "in sackcloth and ashes"? Should we try to take over the world and straighten things out? Should we run to the mountains and escape? The Bible tells us we should *pray*.

What a canned answer! The old "Christian cop-out"— pray! That lets us off the hook, we think, if we put in our

few minutes of prayer time each day. But wait a minute!
After reading the Scripture above we could ask ourselves
a few incriminating questions. Did I pray for the leaders
in the Middle East this week? Did I pray for our President
and my congressman this week?

I feel guilty already, don't you?

Notice the importance of such praying. Verse 1 urges
us to pray on behalf of all men "first of all." So much of
our prayer time is spent on our own personal hang-ups,
our selfish desires, or even our own area of service, that
we only have time to throw in a few token prayers for
others. Now there's nothing wrong with praying about
our personal problems and requests. In fact, we are told
specifically to do that (see Philippians 4:6-7). But here
Scripture is telling us that "first of all" our concern in
prayer should be "on behalf of all men"—that is, others
first and ourselves last.

The "all who are in authority" of verse 2 includes not
only presidents, kings, and dictators, but anyone who is
in a position of authority or prominence and can influence
the masses. That would include political, educational,
industrial, and religious leaders at all levels. We should
pray for the mayors of our cities and the governors of our
states. We should pray for the principals of our high
schools or the presidents of our colleges. We should pray
for church leaders nationally and in our area. We should
pray for national labor leaders as well as our bosses. We
should pray for authors and celebrities, whether famous
or infamous.

What do we pray about? That the leaders of countries
we favor will be given wisdom to win their wars? No!
That the man we support will be elected? No! The end of
verse 2 gives us our answer. "That we may lead a tranquil
and quiet life in all godliness and dignity." Pray for peace
and quiet! But what about the verses like 2 Timothy 3:12
that say a Christian is to expect suffering and persecution?

Yes, that's right, but we are never told to pray for persecution or suffering or trials. We are to pray for peace and quiet. The Bible assures us that world conditions are not going to get any better (see 2 Timothy 3:1), but still we are to pray that the God of all grace would grant a measure of peace and quiet to our lives. "This is good and acceptable in the sight of God our Savior" (1 Timothy 2:3).

Notice that our passage does not in any way suggest that we are to pray for peace and quiet so we can sit around, goof off, and enjoy the good life. We are to pray so we can live godly and dignified lives—peace and quiet for the purpose of worshiping and serving God in all seriousness. Verses 4 and 5 show us that God's *desire* is that all men come to know the truth in Jesus Christ. A godly (what God desires) life for us, then, would also involve concern and action directed toward the goal that mankind come to know Jesus. We are to pray that conditions of life will be such that our worship of Jesus Christ as Lord will be *unharassed* and our service in making Christ known to others will be *unhindered*.

During the persecutions of the early church, Christians could not worship and serve openly. Christians in some countries today cannot worship and serve the Lord in freedom. The world situation is such that, even in this country, conditions of life could change quickly and drastically. And for the openness and freedom we enjoy in our country at the present time we should be *very* thankful to God. (Note the word "thanksgiving" in verse 1.)

So pray that your school administrators will continue to let you talk about Jesus. Pray that your local government will continue to permit Christians to give out the gospel in public. Pray for the salvation of prominent authors and celebrities who influence our society so greatly. Pray that God would give strength, power, and wisdom to the prominent Christian men and women of our time. Pray that decisions made by world leaders in high level councils would allow Christians to "lead a tranquil and quiet life in all godliness and dignity." Pray for peace and quiet!

28

In the Beginning

Genesis 1:1 In the beginning God created the heavens and the earth.
Read Genesis 1-2.

Have you ever noticed that some of your textbooks at school use certain passages of the Bible in support of what they are teaching—but never Genesis 1:1?! For example, your history textbooks (and sociology and anthropology and archaeology) will use the later chapters of Genesis in support of what has been discovered about man's early cultures. But rarely do you find the opening chapters of Genesis even mentioned—except as an example of early legend or myth. Because the content of those chapters flies smack into the face of what modern man wants to believe, that part of the Bible is brushed aside as being unscientific and untrue. Creation is out of the question; a God who creates is an unthinkable concept!

In spite of the attacks by the unbeliever and the ridicule of the skeptics, the first verse in the Bible still stands as the most clear, concise, and beautiful statement of how it all began. And there has never been a better or more logical or more reasonable explanation of what is, than Genesis 1:1. No hypothesis, philosophy, or religion has

come up with a more feasible alternative. From ancient
Babylon's "Enuma Elish" (a polytheistic creation epic
characterized by the grotesque, the mythological, and the
absurd) to modern science's concept of eternal matter,
man has attempted to explain the ever-nagging question
of origins in ways other than the biblical account. However, when all the differing theories are laid out on the
table, there is no opinion or option that can claim *more*
evidence or require *less* faith to believe than the simple
scriptural statement: "In the beginning God created the
heavens and the earth."

The first few words of the Bible are priceless in their
content and importance. They not only convey the truth
of the doctrine of creation but they have also stood as a
bulwark against all kinds of error and heresy. Many
different false concepts of God and nature are refuted.
The belief that God does not exist cannot be true if "In
the beginning God" is true. The Bible does not attempt
to argue philosophically for the existence of God; it
assumes His existence from the start.

It is interesting to notice that those who deny the
existence of God do not really live consistently with their
own belief. In fact, subconsciously, an atheist actually
acknowledges the authority of God every time he judges
something to be morally right or wrong. A consistent
atheist cannot admit moral values, because there is no
such thing as a moral value if there is no God. You see,
an atheist has no real philosophical basis for saying that
you are morally wrong for stealing his car. The most he
can say (and still be consistent with his belief) is that you
have broken a law that has been set up by a majority of
people for the purpose of living more conveniently or
pleasurably. But just let someone try lying to an atheist
or ripping off his books or making time with his mate
and you will see how quickly he becomes a moralist!
Again, rare is the atheist who refuses to admit that Hitler

was *wrong* when he slaughtered six million Jews. But a consistent atheist has no basis for making that judgment. The most he can say (and still be consistent) is that Hitler's action was not *pleasing* to a majority of an animal species on earth known as human beings. Only when God is admitted into the picture do the deeds of Hitler become *evil*. The first words of the Bible bring God into the picture!

Another view that is untenable in the light of Genesis 1:1 is nihilism. Nihilism is the belief that existence is basically useless and senseless because there are no grounds for objective truth. It is the logical outcome of consistent atheism. What possible meaning and purpose can there be in this universe if there are no ultimate realities or absolutes? Many students have felt the despair of nihilism pressing in on them as their belief in God is given up—the result of their expensive quest for "intellectual respectability." As they are sucked into this vortex of despair, they desperately grasp at a flimsy existential "do your own thing" philosophy in the hope that somehow life will take on meaning and purpose. But it is like trying to find meaning in a game of deck tennis on the sinking Titanic! What a difference an acceptance of the first verse of the Bible makes. The words, "God created the heavens and the earth," not only show that there are real and objective grounds for truth, but they also introduce us to the truth that there is meaning and purpose in this universe. As the biblical narrative unfolds, we learn who God is, as well as His plan and purpose for His creation.

Another idea opposed by the first words of the Bible is a radical materialism, a theory that holds that matter is eternal. This view assumes that there is nothing more than matter in this mechanical universe. Man is but a part of a complex machine. There is *nothing* spiritual; only molecules of matter explain it all. Man is no better than the material chair he sits on—just a "higher" and more complex arrangement of molecules.

The radical materialist is forced to his *faith* in the eternity of matter by the first law of thermodynamics. That law (which is known even by high school students taking General Science) states that energy can change its form but not its quantity. That is, the amount of energy within the universe is constant, even though it can vary in form. For example, when we put gasoline in our cars the chemical energy of the gas is converted to mechanical work as well as heat and noise, but no energy is lost or gained—it is just changed in form. Einstein's famous equation showed that all matter in the universe can be equated to energy. That energy may take various forms, but no energy is now being created or destroyed. What does the first law of thermodynamics say about our material universe? It says that the universe cannot have created itself—either it was created or it is eternal. Those are the only two rational options. The radical materialist opts for the latter. The first words of the Bible permit only one possibility: the "heavens and the earth" were created.

Although the first law of thermodynamics seems to leave the door open for either of the above options, the second law of thermodynamics comes down pretty hard on the radical materialist. The second law states that in any "closed system" there is always a tendency to disorder and decay. Living things die; machinery wears out; buildings crumble; stars burn up. Yes, there are "events" of increasing order such as the development of an automobile on an assembly line or the development of an embryo within a womb. Those examples seem to contradict the second law of thermodynamics, but it is only because they are "open systems" where "outside help" is being given to them. They are but "pockets" of increasing order within larger closed systems where the overall tendency is toward disintegration. Our sun is burning up at a certain rate and cannot last forever. Without "outside help" (and the Bible has a lot to say about that!), the universe would eventually run down. It logically follows, then, that some time in the past the material universe was "wound up" and more ordered than it is now. The second law strongly hints (it even twists your arm!) that there was a beginning to this universe—it is not eternal, and it must have been created.

The first and second laws of thermodynamics are solid scientific statements. They *demand* a beginning and a Creator for this universe. Far-out ideas, such as an eternally cyclic universe, are but cop-outs to get around the *laws* of thermodynamics. Ironically, it takes just as much faith (if not more!) to accept those ideas as it does to accept the words of Genesis 1:1.

A host of other "-isms" are also put down by the first few words in the Bible. Polytheism, pantheism, dualism, and naturalism are but a few of the many concepts of God and nature that oppose the teaching of the first verse of the Word of God. Your school textbooks may contain a lot of good stuff, but remember that the *first* words in the greatest Textbook of all are: "In the beginning God created the heavens and the earth."

29

Catch the Foxes

Song of Solomon 2:15 Catch the foxes for us, the little foxes that are ruining the vineyards, while our vineyards are in blossom.
Read all of Song of Solomon.

Spring is the time of year when everything bursts into bloom—including love. The cold, bitter winds and bare branches disappear. The warm, light breezes and colorful blossoms arrive. Budding life and love are everywhere. It's great to be alive! How welcome is that walk in the park or through the woods—especially when you're walking with that special person.

Hey, wait a minute! What does all this "love in the springtime" talk have to do with the Bible? Well, the Bible does have a lot to say about love between the sexes—including budding romances. In fact, the entire book of Song of Solomon is about love and romance. As for the title above, you can see from our text that it is taken straight from the Bible. We'll see below that the phrase "catching foxes" is a figurative expression for something important about a love relationship. (Incidentally, the phrase doesn't have anything to do with chasing the opposite sex!) But before we get down to "catching foxes," let's talk a little about the Song of Solomon in general.

Some growing Christians have never even read Song of Solomon, let alone been able to understand the book. And those Christians who *have* read and studied the book know that all Bible scholars and commentators are not agreed on exactly how the Song should be interpreted. Some say that there were just two lovers in the story, while others say that three lovers were involved.

The three-lover (or triangular) view was first put forward in the late 1700s and is thus relatively recent in church history. In this view, the true love affair was not between King Solomon and the Shulammite maiden, but rather between the young woman and her shepherd boyfriend. The Shulammite (maybe from the area of Shunem in the north of Israel) and the shepherd were just simple country folk who had fallen in love and were planning on marriage. But along came the "villain," King Solomon. When he caught a glimpse of the beautiful maiden, he lusted after her and abducted her for his already large (6:8) royal harem. But, in spite of all his wooing and wealth, Solomon could not persuade the Shulammite maiden to give in to him. She remained true to her shepherd fiancé and continued to talk and dream only of him. In the meantime, her shepherd lover came to Jerusalem to see what he could do to get his fiancée released from Solomon's clutches. Finally, Solomon granted the Shulammite woman her freedom. She and her shepherd then traveled home to the country together, happily looking forward to their marriage.

In the traditional two-lover view of the Song, we have the historical account of King Solomon's true love for the Shulammite peasant girl. Solomon had observed this beautiful woman while on a trip in the northern territories of his kingdom—maybe during a visit to certain crown property or vineyards. The Shulammite woman was working nearby in her own family's vineyard (1:6) when Solomon spied her. She had no idea that she was soon to become Cinderella. Rather than use his powers as king to abduct the maiden for his harem, Solomon decided to disguise himself as a shepherd and win her heart by slowly building a love relationship with her.

The plan worked! Soon Solomon revealed his identity to her, and shortly thereafter the couple was married. King Solomon, of course, spared no expense for the wedding. The marriage procession is described in all its splendor at the end of chapter 3; the wedding takes place within chapter 4; the marriage is consummated at the beginning of chapter 5. In the context of the royal palace and in the public eye, the love relationship between Solomon and his bride continues to deepen and mature throughout the rest of the Song.

That does not mean, however, that the story closes with a few "lived happily ever after" lines. No, this is not some fairy tale, but a real life story—even though it is written in poetic form. In chapter 5, for example, there is a little misunderstanding between the lovers. And at the end of chapter 7 and the beginning of chapter 8, the Shulammite woman appears to be a little uptight with all the demands of public life in the royal palace. She would much rather have had Solomon all to herself back in the simple village where she had been raised. Oh, to be free from all the social proprieties and taboos against the public display of affection, and be able to kiss her husband in public—like a brother (8:1).

But in spite of those ripples, the love between husband and wife continued to grow. Their love triumphed over the misunderstandings. They did not let the little frustrations gnaw away at their relationship. If only *we* worked at our love relationships in the same way—our love for the Lord, our love for that special person God has given or is giving us, our love for one another! That is precisely where the work of "catching little foxes" becomes important.

The statement about foxes comes near the end of what appears, in the Song, to be a spring walk in the hills with all the beauty of nature bursting out everywhere (2:10-13). The lovers then resolve to work at their relationship and not let anything come in to spoil its beauty. They liken potential problem areas in their blossoming romance to little foxes. As little foxes can ruin the vineyards by gnawing at the tender shoots, so can the little problems that inevitably show up in a growing love relationship ruin that relationship. Those little foxes must be caught and stopped before they do further damage.

Little foxes always seem to come around just when we're getting it all together in our love relationships—when the "vineyards are in blossom." Take our love relationship with the Lord, for example. Just when everything seems to be going well, the little fox of neglect shows up—neglect of daily reading of God's Word or neglect of regular prayer time. And what about our relationship with that particular person of the opposite sex that the Lord has picked out for us? How often the little foxes of cutting words cause needless breakdowns in relationships that could otherwise be so beautiful. And then there are the little foxes of petty jealousies and mini-misunderstandings that tear down our love for one another. How sad! Without some definite "catching" action on our part, the *little* foxes will continue to eat away until they become *big* foxes!

Regardless of which view is taken of Song of Solomon, many such applications can be made from the story. Even if the phrase "catch the foxes" is to be interpreted differently (one interpretation holds that these are the words of the Shulammite brothers who are telling their sister to stop her daydreaming and literally get back to the family vineyard to protect the vines from the foxes), the story is still loaded with lessons for us because it is a love story. In any love relationship presented in the Bible there are many valuable lessons that are applicable to our own love relationships. Probably the greatest lesson that we can learn from Song of Solomon is that sex is OK. Sex is not a "no-no" or only a necessary means to propagate the human race. No, physical love between husband and wife is a wonderful God-given gift. As long as it is within the bounds that God has set up (and the Bible clearly gives us the boundary markers), sex is beautiful.

Because the Song portrays the deep and wonderful love between man and woman, it obviously becomes a beautiful illustration of the love relationship between Christ and His people. God has ordained that the love relationship between man and his bride should reflect the love relationship between Christ and *His* Bride, the church (Ephesians 5:31-32). What a tremendous testimony for the Lord your marriage will be if you determine from the start that it is going to reflect that wonderful mystery of our Lord's love for us! That will involve a lot of hard work, because a lot of "foxes" will have to be caught. Don't let the little foxes spoil the message God wants to convey through *your* marriage.

Sly little foxes are not always easy to catch, but the job is not impossible. The problem areas that are bound to come in every growing love relationship are not always easy to "catch," but with diligent effort and divine assistance, the task is not insurmountable.

30

Endure Hardships

2 Timothy 4:5 But you, be sober in all things, endure hardship, do the work of an evangelist, fulfill your ministry.

Read all of 2 Timothy 4.

"What does the future hold for me?" Perhaps a lot of you are asking that question right about now, in view of the end of the school year and graduation. Some of you know what you're going to do this summer and next September, and some of you don't have the faintest idea yet. Well, regardless of the timing and details of God's plan for you individually, we can be sure of one thing about God's future program for every growing Christian. There will be hardships! Now that statement is not meant to be a wet blanket on your enthusiasm; rather, it is meant to be a stabilizer. Knowing that hardships will come in our lives should help to preserve us from the trauma of "hardship shock." It is especially important for growing Christians to realize that hardships are a definite part of God's plan for our lives.

In 2 Timothy 4:5 the apostle Paul encouraged Timothy to endure the hardships that would continue to come in Timothy's future. That was part of the overall charge (v.

1) that Paul gave to Timothy as he prepared himself for martyrdom (vv. 6-7). Soon after Paul penned this last letter from prison, he was with the Lord. The hardships were finally over for Paul. In view of "that day" (v. 8), Timothy was to endure hardships as part of his earthly ministry. The charge to endure hardships until the Lord's return is for all Christians (v. 8).

The hardships that Paul specifically had in mind when he wrote verse 5 were not the average kind of day-to-day hassles that confront us. Christians and non-Christians alike have those—like losing an important homework assignment or ripping a pair of good jeans or blowing it big in front of everyone. No, the hardships in view here are those difficulties that particularly affect Christians who are trying to be faithful to the Lord. It is possible to be a Christian without going through any more hardships than the average "man on the street." *But* it's a different story if we want to meet the Lord as a "good and faithful slave" (Matthew 25:21). In that case there are additional hardships that come our way because of our open and verbal identification with the Lord Jesus. And the Bible leaves no doubt that those kinds of hardships will come to the faithful Christian (see 2 Timothy 3:12, for example). We are not to be surprised if the going is tough in this world (see 1 John 3:13). Those "extra" hardships are all part of what it means to be "bearing His reproach" (Hebrews 13:13). We are not to try to escape hardships by running from them or compromising our testimony. We are to *endure hardships!*

What are some of those special hardships that a faithful Christian may be called upon to endure? In verses 9-16 of our chapter the apostle mentions several hardships that he was experiencing as a result of faithfulness to Christ. Perhaps the Lord will call on us to undergo similar hardships in the near future. Will we be faithful and endure?

In verse 9 we detect the hardship of *loneliness*. Paul was lonely in that Roman dungeon. Because of his faithful witness for the Lord, Paul was even deprived of normal Christian fellowship. Doctor Luke was in the area (v. 11), but Paul yearned for the fellowship of Timothy, his close companion and son in the faith (see also 1 Timothy 1:2). God may permit us to go through the hardship of loneliness. Although the availability of lots of fellow Christians is the norm in our Christian experience, there are times when God takes us through the valley of loneliness. Here we learn to appreciate the value of Christian fellowship. Here we experience (maybe for the first time) the reality of the Lord's constant and comforting personal presence. Loneliness may come in military service when you are the only Christian in your unit. You may experience loneliness in the new job or location where you're headed. College and graduate school can be very lonely places if no Christian fellowship is immediately available. Are we willing to undergo the hardship of loneliness for the sake of Christ—even the absence of fellowship with those Christian friends who have meant so much to us in the past?

The hardship of *desertion* is mentioned in verse 10. Demas had been one of Paul's fellow-workers (Colossians 4:14 and Philemon 24). But Demas could not resist the appeal of what this world had to offer, and he deserted the apostle Paul. Maybe it was a lucrative job offer in Thessalonica that was just "too good" to turn down. Maybe Demas was feeling burned out in the ministry and just wanted to settle down and live a "normal" life. In any case, Demas became a deserter because he "loved this present world." (Notice how that "love" contrasts with that of those who "loved His appearing" at the end of verse 8.) What a disappointment for Paul! It wasn't that Demas had given up the faith or defected doctrinally like Hymenaeus and Philetus (2 Timothy 2:17-18). No, it was that Demas had let the values and attitudes of this world system govern his life-style more and more. What a difference between Demas and the other fellow-workers mentioned in verses 10-12. Crescens, Titus, Luke, Mark, and Tychicus were all hanging in there and faithfully serving the Lord in various parts of the Roman Empire.

The hardship Paul experienced when Demas deserted was not just the loss of much needed help. It was also the discouragement of losing a personal friend and colleague and *fellow*-worker. Not only had Paul expended valuable time and energy in training Demas, but he had come to know and love Demas as a brother in the Lord. It hurts to have a faithful friend and disciple whom you have trained and worked with turn his back on you and desert you. It is disheartening to see a promising fellow believer walk away from your counsel and teaching and go "do his own thing." And yet that is one of the hardships that we can expect along the way. Remember our Lord Jesus experienced the same hurt when one of His disciples deserted Him. In view of the many and varied opportunities that this world has to offer, we must be extremely careful not to become like Demas ourselves.

Another hardship is seen in verse 13. It involves the area of *personal needs*. Paul suffered from the needs of the body as well as the needs of the mind. With winter coming on (v. 21), Paul needed his heavy cloak to keep warm in that cold and damp Roman dungeon. The apostle also desired the books and the parchments to meet the needs of his mind. Most likely the parchment scrolls were portions of the Old Testament Scriptures, and the books (papyrus sheets or rolls) may even have included some recently written New Testament portions. Paul never stopped studying, even when he was in prison awaiting death!

This one verse alone should convince us that the life of the growing Christian should always include the dedi-

cated study of the Word of God. And that goes for
Christians who have just graduated from school and are
very excited about new opportunities and very involved
in new situations! Although the needs of our bodies and
minds are usually more than adequately cared for, sometimes the Lord calls upon us to go through a special
period of testing in this area. Faithful Christians down
through history have been deprived of personal needs
because of their witness for Christ. The Word of God has
even been taken away from some faithful believers. God
may not call upon us to endure that kind of hardship for
His sake, but let us at least remember to pray for our
brothers and sisters around the world who are even now
suffering personal need for the sake of Jesus Christ.

A further hardship that Paul mentions is *open opposition* (vv. 14-15). Alexander the coppersmith took every
opportunity he could to oppose the apostle and his
teaching. He may have been the "Alexander" of 1 Timothy 1:20, and in view of verse 16, he may have been the
main accuser of Paul before the imperial court. Opposition to our ministry and personal harm is not an indication that we are out of the Lord's will. It is a hardship
that will inevitably come if we are faithfully verbalizing
the gospel of Jesus Christ—on the job or on the campus.
Opposition should not cause us to become bitter, frustrated, or revengeful. Although we are to be on guard
(watch and beware) against such opposition (v. 15), we
are to leave vengeance to the Lord (v. 14; Romans 12:19).

One more hardship is given in verse 16. It was the
matter of *no support* at the preliminary hearing of the
trial. Apparently none of the Christians in Rome was
willing to risk his neck to stand up for Paul. (Faithful
Luke probably had not arrived in time for the first
defense.) We too can expect the hardship of no support
from fellow Christians when risk is involved. In times of
danger some Christians have a way of disappearing when

you desperately need their support. After all, their reputation or position or security may be involved! We are to
endure this hardship also, and even pray the prayer of
forgiveness for those who don't support us (v. 16).

We can be sure that the Lord will support us when
others leave us stranded (v. 17). It seems that Paul was
supernaturally strengthened with enough courage to fearlessly proclaim the gospel before the Imperial Tribunal.
Talk about courage! And Paul was supernaturally delivered from the "mouth of the lion"—most likely a figurative expression for Nero or Satan (1 Peter 5:8) or great
danger in general. The Lord can make us bold for the
gospel too—even in the presence of unbelieving professors or bosses! There really is no need to fear, because
God can bring deliverance in any situation, regardless of
the support or nonsupport of other believers.

Ultimately the Lord will deliver us out of this earthly
scene of hardships and bring us safely to Himself forever
(v. 18). Until then we are to expect and endure hardships.

SUMMER

31

Summer First Fruits

James 1:18-25 In the exercise of His will He brought us forth by the word of truth, so that we might be, as it were, the first fruits among His creatures. This you know, my beloved brethren. But let every one be quick to hear, slow to speak and slow to anger; for the anger of man does not achieve the righteousness of God. Therefore putting aside all filthiness and all that remains of wickedness, in humility receive the word implanted, which is able to save your souls. But prove yourselves doers of the word, and not merely hearers who delude themselves. For if any one is a hearer of the word and not a doer, he is like a man who looks at his natural face in a mirror; for once he has looked at himself and gone away, he has immediately forgotten what kind of person he was. But one who looks intently at the perfect law, the law of liberty, and abides by it, not having become a forgetful hearer but an effectual doer, this man shall be blessed in what he does.

In New England the blossoms of spring are "still hanging in there" on the fruit trees. They are not only very beautiful, but they are a promise of the harvest to come. The firstfruits of summer will soon be here!

Christians are a kind of firstfruits. Verse 18 of our Scripture tells us that God "brought us forth" by His Word to be "first fruits among His creatures." That is, God planted the good seed of His Word in the responsive ground of our hearts; He saw that seed take root in our lives; He carefully watered and cultivated us; He watched us blossom in the springtime of our new life in Christ; and now He desires "that we might be" firstfruits of the summer harvest.

We are firstfruits because the harvest has only begun. The Word of God makes clear that some day all creation will be subject to the Lord Jesus Christ (Romans 8:18-23). Every growing Christian is a firstfruit of this great harvest. In the Old Testament (Leviticus 23:10) the firstfruits of the summer harvest were presented to the Lord as a sacrifice in gratitude for His goodness and in recognition of His faithfulness. So we have the idea of dedication also in the term "first fruits." (See Romans 12:1 for the concept of *presenting* ourselves as a living *sacrifice*.)

The rest of our passage speaks about hearing, receiving, and doing the Word of God. What does that have to do with firstfruits? Just this! If the seed that brought forth the firstfruits was the Word of God, then certainly the Word of God should characterize the firstfruits. When you plant an apple seed you expect the fruit to be apples, not grapes! "Like seed, like fruit," is what God is teaching us. How can we be characterized by the Word of God, the very seed that begot us? Answer: hear and receive God's Word (James 1:19-21); hear and obey God's Word (vv. 22-25).

Verses 19-21 tell us to make a deliberate effort to split from sin and then to *receive* the implanted Word. Implanted means it is already there! It is the very seed planted by God that resulted in our new birth (1 Peter 1:23). But now we are to hear and *receive* the Word. A

Christian hasn't really received a particular portion of God's Word until it begins to transform his life. For example, you haven't received the Twenty-third Psalm if you are still "wanting." To want your own way, to be frustrated about your future, or to be frustrated with your lot in life are to deny and not receive "The Lord is my Shepherd, *I shall not want*" (Psalm 23:1). We are to receive the Word in humility, with meekness (James 1:21). We must be willing to submit and let God change us through His Word. In this way the Word saves our souls; that is, God uses His Word not only to save our souls from eternal *damnation* but also from present *damage*. When we hear and receive the words of Scripture our lives begin to be transformed from the inside out.

Verses 22-25 tell us to be *doers* of the Word—obedience to God's Word! If we are firstfruits, we are to be characterized by the Word of God—inside and out. To *hear and receive* is to be characterized internally and subjectively by the Word; to *hear and obey* is to be characterized externally and objectively by it.

In response to the Great Commission (Matthew 28:18-20) for example, we may be really "into" the Word of God, but until we begin to verbalize the gospel to our roommates or neighbors and until we're actively involved in discipling and teaching someone, we are not *hearing and obeying* the Word of God—in fact, we are deceiving ourselves (v. 22). Only when our external life-styles begin to change for the cause of Christ can we consider ourselves obedient to the Word. Up to that point we are like someone who hurries past a mirror (vv. 23-24). How can a brief look at a two-dimensional reflection possibly change us? But when we look intently (v. 25) into God's perfect Word and obey it, then our lives themselves begin to reflect the glory of God.

And that's where the blessing is! The end of verse 25 tells us that we are blessed when we *do;* not when we merely hear. Do you want to know the love and blessing and joy of God in your life? Then stop wishing and start obeying! That is exactly what the Lord Jesus tells us in John 15:10-11: "If you keep My commandments, you will abide in My love; just as I have kept My Father's commandments, and abide in His love. These things I have spoken to you, that My joy may be in you, and that your joy may be made full."

Soon we will see the summer firstfruits in the fields and orchards all over this country. In your travels this summer, let the sight of the fulfillment of nature remind you that we too are firstfruits for our Lord. Let us be characterized by His holy Word inside and out. What a disappointment it must be to God if, after a beautiful blossom, the fruit turns out to be spoiled and marred.

32

Comfortable or Comforted?

2 Corinthians 1:3-4 Blessed be the God and Father of our Lord Jesus Christ, the Father of mercies and God of all comfort; who comforts us in all our affliction so that we may be able to comfort those who are in any affliction with the comfort with which we ourselves are comforted by God.
Read 2 Corinthians 1:3-11.

What comes to your mind when the word *comfort* is mentioned? A hammock in the summer shade with a gentle breeze blowing and a pitcher of cold lemonade nearby? A reclining chair beside the fire in a cozy den on a cold winter day? Those are not what the Bible means by comfort.

In order to catch the biblical meaning of the word, picture in your mind the following situations: a struggling swimmer being rescued by a strong lifeguard; a sobbing child, lost in the supermarket, being helped by a kind store manager; a grief-stricken mother being consoled by a compassionate pastor; an accused citizen being assisted by an able defense lawyer. (The word "advocate" in 1 John 2:1 is the same word translated "comforter" in John 14-16, where the Lord Jesus refers to the Holy

Spirit.) You see, in the Bible the primary idea in the word "comfort" is "to come alongside of," to give aid in time of need. That is really what comfort is all about.

Verse 3 tells us that our God is a God of comfort. He is not a hard and unconcerned boss but rather a helping and supporting, compassionate, and consoling Father who "comes alongside" to help in times of trouble. He is the "Father of mercies and God of all comfort" (2 Corinthians 1:3). *All* comfort ultimately has its source in God. Why, then, in times of need, do we look within ourselves to find a source of comfort? It's just not there! It's pretty hard to "come alongside of" yourself to help yourself! The source of all comfort resides outside of ourselves in God. David said, "I will lift up my eyes. . . . My help comes from the Lord" (Psalm 121:1-2). David knew that it was useless to look within himself for help. All his help came from without—from the Lord Himself.

The first part of verse 4 contains a promise we may claim: our heavenly Father will comfort us in *all* our affliction. The word "affliction" here means "pressed or burdened of spirit." It does not mean only physical suffering but *anything* that comes along to get us down— like the pressure of circumstances or the antagonism of people. God has promised to come alongside us and help us during *all* those times. So let's claim that promise! Do you feel like tossing in the towel right now because nobody appreciates the job you're doing? Claim the promise and call on the Lord. Does it seem as if everyone is picking on you and no one understands? Look to the Lord. He has promised to "come alongside" and comfort you.

Now a word of qualification is in order here. The Bible tells us that we should call on the Lord "from a pure heart" (2 Timothy 2:22). In other words, if our spirits are pressed because we are bitter against God or angry with our folks or jealous of our roommates, then we should not expect God to come alongside and comfort us. Most likely He will discipline us (in love, of course). But if our hearts are right, then we can *always* count on God to "come alongside" and help us in our times of need.

Another beautiful side of this promise in verse 4 is that *He* will comfort us in all our afflictions. A problem for *us* is what is pressing in on our spirits. Someone else may consider that burden insignificant, or it may be too personal to discuss with anyone; but it is pressure on our spirits just the same. If we call on the Lord we can be sure that He will come alongside us to give us aid. We must admit that we do make mountains out of molehills and we do mix up our priorities. Many of our problems are our own faults—but still, God, in His grace, comes alongside and helps us in our problems. What a promise!

The second half of verse 4 speaks of the responsibility given to Christians who have known the comfort of God: we are to comfort others! The comfort of God is not to dead-end with us; we are to pass it along! That is the very personal method by which God has chosen to distribute His comfort. We are to come near to others who are in need and give them comfort. We are not comforted to be comfortable, but to be comforters.

We see, then, that one of the reasons God permits us to go through troubles and hardships is to open up "comfort channels" for others. Did you ever experience the comfort of God when you were lonely? Then go to that lonely student down the hall and pass on the comfort of God. Did God "come alongside of" you and bridge the troubled waters when you and the one you had dated for two years broke up? Then "come alongside of" that heartbroken friend who needs the comfort that only God can give. Was the Lord there to help you when you lost your job? Then "come alongside of" your neighbor who has just been laid off, and let God comfort him through you. You have become a channel of comfort! We are not to avoid people who have problems, we are to get involved—to "comfort those who are in any affliction with the comfort with which we ourselves are comforted by God" (v. 4).

Many Christians think that the ideal life is one that is completely free of problems or afflictions—just one, big, comfortable ride. They even get a little angry with God when things don't go smoothly, and feel that God is "letting them down." But if our lives were free of problems, we would never know the comfort of God. The ideal life for the growing Christian is not one that is comfortable—it is one that is comforted—and comforting.

33

We Are One in the Spirit

Ephesians 4:2-6 Be completely humble and gentle;
be patient, bearing with one another in love. Make
every effort to keep the unity of the Spirit through the
bond of peace. There is one body and one Spirit—just
as you were called to one hope when you were
called—one Lord, one faith, one baptism; one God
and Father of all, who is over all and through all and
in all (NIV).

The lyrics of a well-known Christian song begin with
the emphatic declaration that "We are one in the Spirit."
But the song continues with a prayer for the restoration
of our unity. In some ways the words of that familiar
song seem like a contradiction, don't they? Why pray for
unity to be restored, if we *are* one in the Spirit already?
Actually the words are right! They express at the same
time both a profound Christian truth and a great Christian
responsibility. The truth is that we *are* one in the Spirit,
and the responsibility is that that unity is to be seen in
our lives.

What exactly is our unity, and how are we to show it in
our lives? Should we attempt to break down all the
denominational barriers and start a new denomination—

"The Church for All True Christians"? Needless to say, such a plan would hardly get off the ground without serious and divisive consequences. And yet we are told to *make every effort* to keep the unity of the Spirit (v. 3).

A closer examination of Ephesians 4:2-6 will help to answer these questions. Notice first of all that verse 3 does not say "make every effort to *form* the unity of the Spirit." Why not? Because the unity of the Spirit is something which is already formed. We *are* one in the Spirit. No amount of ecumenical maneuvering can add a thing to the unity that God has already formed.

Now in verses 4-6 we have the basis or the ground of our unity in the Spirit, a sevenfold oneness: "There is one body . . . one Spirit . . . one hope . . . one Lord, one faith, one baptism, one God." Notice again that unity is not something that *we* form. "There *is*" is understood throughout. We cannot add to or take away from the oneness that already *is*.

To better appreciate the essential ingredients of our unity in the Spirit, visualize three concentric spheres. Label the outer sphere with the words of verse 6: "one God and Father of all." Label the middle sphere with verse 5: "one Lord, one faith, one baptism." Finally, label the inner sphere with verse 4: "one body . . . one Spirit . . . one hope." Although all seven aspects of our oneness are essential (all are contained within the larger sphere), it is as we move from the outer sphere toward the inner one that we come to the heart of our unity. Non-Christians as well as Christians may subscribe to "one God," but only true Christians are members of the Body of Christ and have the Holy Spirit.

Let's look at these three spheres in more detail. "There is . . . one God and Father of all, who is over all and through all and in all" (v. 6). God is Creator of all. He has authority over all. He sustains all and is in control of all. His presence is everywhere. All Christians hold this truth, but then so do many others—even Moslems! But there is more to our unity, as seen in the middle sphere: "One Lord, one faith, one baptism" (v. 5). All Christians believe that Jesus alone is Lord. We hold to one faith as taught in the Holy Scriptures. Although we may differ on interpretations of some passages, together we "contend earnestly for the faith which was once for all delivered to the saints" (Jude 3). (See 1 Corinthians 15:3-4 for the content of the one faith.) What about one baptism? Is it "Spirit baptism" or "water baptism"? Most likely it is water baptism, because the Spirit is mentioned as we move further in toward the center, but water baptism certainly symbolizes what the Spirit has done in our lives. Notice that it doesn't say "one *mode* of baptism." Christians may differ as to the mode, but all agree that Christian baptism has one basic meaning—I belong to Christ!

The inner sphere shows us that our unity is even deeper than the confession of Lord, faith, and baptism. "There is one body" (Ephesians 4:4). All true Christians are joined in the one Body of Christ. He is the Head of that Body (4:15-16). It doesn't matter whether we are Congregational or Catholic or "common Christian." If we love the Lord Jesus, we *are* part of that one Body. It is not an organization that *we* join or *we* maintain—it is a living organism that God has created. "There is . . . one Spirit" (4:4). Although there are many different spiritual gifts and manifestations (1 Corinthians 12:4-11), there is only one Holy Spirit. Regardless of how we view those spiritual gifts and manifestations, all Christians are one in *the* Spirit. Finally, only true Christians can claim the "one hope" of sharing Christ's glory forever (Ephesians 1:18). This then is the basis of our unity in the Spirit. It is true that non-Christians may subscribe to one God, and some confessing Christians may even profess faith and undergo baptism (Matthew 7:21-23), but the Spirit indwells only the one Body of true believers.

Yes, we really are one in the Spirit, and nothing can destroy the unity that God Himself has formed. But we are told to "make every effort to keep [or preserve] the unity of the Spirit" (Ephesians 4:3). How? As individual members of the one Body of Christ we do everything possible to recognize and reflect our oneness in Christ. We may differ in our views of when and how our Lord is going to return. We may differ in our concepts of church government. We may differ in our ideas of spiritual gifts for the church today. But we are not to let those things keep us from recognizing one another as brothers and sisters in the Lord. Those things are not the ground of our unity. Members of an earthly family can hold different opinions but still exhibit the family unity in love, because *they are one* family. How much more should we who are members of the *one Body* (not just family) of Christ reflect our unity in "the bond of peace" (v. 3)?

Keeping the unity of the Spirit is more easily said than done! True, but we are to "make every effort" (v. 3). How do we start? Verse 2 shows us that we begin with ourselves and then move out to others. "Be completely humble and gentle." We become humble when we begin to see ourselves as God sees us. Our natural tendency is to see ourselves as the "star" we would like to be. God sees the motives and the masks. Gentle is sometimes translated as "meek." Meekness is not an easy-going weakness but is the result of a mind and spirit kept under control. We are to make every effort to be gentle. "Be patient," or, "long-suffering" (v. 2). That involves others besides ourselves! Someone has said that "long-suffering is the spirit that can suffer unpleasant people with graciousness and fools without complaint." Yes, there are such people even in the Body of Christ!

We should be "bearing with one another in love" (v. 2). This goes even further than patience. We are not just to tolerate our brothers and sisters, but actually to love them in their weaknesses. Love involves helping—not despising or judging. "With one another" clearly indicates that we *all* have our shortcomings. We must bear with one another in love, in spite of our different life-styles, opinions, and hang-ups. It is as we make every effort to love one another that the unity of the Spirit is kept in the bond of peace.

It is not easy to keep the unity of the Spirit. Even so, as people who *are* one in the Holy Spirit, we are called to be holy people. It is hard work, but the Spirit who makes us one Body also empowers the new life He gives us. Keeping the unity of the Spirit is not an impossibility! Let us make every effort to show that we are one in the Spirit.

34

Worship is a Way of Life

Mark 14:7 For the poor you always have with you, and whenever you wish, you can do them good; but you do not always have Me.
Read Mark 14:3-9. (Read also the parallel accounts in Matthew 25:6-13 and John 12:1-8.)

Some Christians have the idea that worship is only possible in the sanctuary of a church, that it consists only of flowery phrases, pouring forth spontaneously from the mouth, and that it takes place only when beautiful warm feelings flood the soul. It is true that a lot of Christians have some warped ideas about what worship is all about.

When we look at all of the Scriptures touching on the subject of worship, we find we can sum it up in the following way—worship acknowledges who God is and what God does, and it is directed to God Himself. That acknowledgment must be from the heart—not just some outward mechanical religious motions. True worship without love is inconceivable.

Our acknowledgment may be given by lip or by life. That is, worship may be either verbal praises and thanksgivings to God for who He is and what He does, or it may be nonverbal deeds done in such acknowledgment. A Christian student who, out of recognition of God's standards, refuses to lower his or her moral standards, in spite of ridicule, is worshiping the Lord. His way of life acknowledges God's standards of holiness. A Christian who, without anger or bitterness, accepts from God what others label as tragedy, also is worshiping the Lord. He is acknowledging God's sovereignty and His claims over life. Nonverbal worship is far more acceptable in God's sight than mere "mouthing" of prayers and praises on Sunday mornings—from otherwise complaining lips and compromising lives (see Isaiah 1:10-17).

The ideal, of course, is to have all of our words and actions characterized by worship—in the crucible of life, as well as in the church setting. Worship is not just one of several categories in the Christian life. It is the sum total of living as a Christian.

The woman's anointing of the Lord Jesus (Mark 14:3-9) reveals various aspects of worship. We believe that the woman was Mary of Bethany—the one who sat and learned the Word of God at the Lord's feet in Luke 10:39 (see the parallel account in John 12:1-8). Mary's act of worship can teach us lots about our own worship.

Worship involves sacrifice! A lot of hard work and sacrifice went into Mary's worship. Pure nard was a very expensive perfume, imported all the way from India. Three hundred denarii (Mark 14:5) was about a year's wages for the average working man in those days. Does *my* worship of God cost me anything, or is it just "cheap perfume" involving no sacrifice? Will my worship this summer, for example, require any sacrifice of time for the Lord—or will my summer just be all of the "fun in the sun" I can get for myself?

Mary's action of pouring perfume over the Lord's head should not be questioned as improper or "far-out." It was the common practice in that dry and dusty climate for guests to have their feet washed and their heads anointed with oil. What *is* unusual here, however, is that Mary did not use common, ordinary anointing oil, but very costly perfume. Mary's action was extraordinary—think of what she could have done with three hundred denarii. Yet, in one act, she sacrificed it all, out of love for her Lord. Think of what we could do with a year's salary! Are we willing to sacrifice that much—at one time—for our Lord? Worship is sacrifice (see Hebrews 13:15-16 and Romans 12:1). How much is our worship costing us?

Worship does not hold back; it "goes all out." It is possible to sacrifice some, but still only "go halfway." Look at Mary's action. The Lord was a dinner guest in the home of Simon the leper. (Perhaps he was one of those healed by the Lord.) It seems that Mary, her brother Lazarus, and her sister Martha were also guests. In the course of the meal, Mary came up to the Lord's couch, broke open the alabaster flask, and poured the entire contents of expensive perfume over the Lord—John 12:3 tells us that it was an entire pound. Pure nard was a light and volatile liquid perfume that would quickly evaporate and leave no mess. No wonder "the house was filled with the fragrance of the ointment" (John 12:3). Mary did not hold back in her act of worship. She did not anoint the Lord with only a few drops of her precious possession. She did not use half of the perfume and keep the rest for herself. She gave Him the whole thing! That is worship at its highest.

The Lord responded to her. "She has done what she could" (Mark 14:8). The full force of His statement is lost in our English translations. It sounds as if Jesus is saying, "Well, Mary couldn't do much, but she did what little she could." What the Lord is actually saying is that Mary did *all* that she could. She went to the limit of her ability—she "went all out!" What about us? Does the Lord have to say that we have done "a *few* drops" of what

we could, or *half* of what we could, or can He say that we
have done *all* that we could possibly do? What about my
plans for my future and my intended career? Am I holding anything back from God for just *me?* Worship does
not hold back—it "goes all out."

Worship is not a waste of time and effort. We read that
some of the guests—Judas, as well as the other disciples
(John 12:4-5 and Matthew 26:8)—were disturbed with
Mary's act of worship. They called it wasteful and said
the money would have been better spent in relief for the
poor (Mark 14:4-5). After all, a year's salary can go a long
way in meeting the needs of the poor. Why waste the
money on a flask of expensive perfume, when ordinary
anointing oil would have done the job? Perhaps Mary
was caught up in the emotion of the moment and should
have been more restrained. But such reasoning was squelched
by the Lord. He not only defended Mary's action but
commended her for it (v. 6).

Many people today find fault with Christians who
"waste" their time and efforts in prayer and praise while
the crying needs of the world surround us. How can we
justify spending time celebrating the Lord's Supper, for
example, when children are starving in our own city?
Jesus does not tell them to forget the needs of the poor in
worshiping Him. Instead, He encourages them to make a
constant effort to meet those constant needs (v. 7). In fact,
meeting the needs of the poor in the name of Christ *is*
worship, acknowledging to God His care and concern for
His creatures. (How is our worship in this area?) But to
care for the poor *only*, without an expressed love for
Christ is to neglect worship—that is wrong for the Christian. Some growing Christians tend to become unbalanced,
in either direction, at this point. Proper integration is to
constantly give thanks to the Lord for everything and to
constantly let that praise ripple out in our actions for the
benefit of others.

The depth of Mary's worship is further revealed in verse 8. What does the Lord mean when He says, "She has anointed My body beforehand for the burial"? Mary knew that the Lord was about to give up His life. She may have understood our Lord's teaching about His death and resurrection more than the other believers—even the disciples (see Mark 8:31-33 and 9:31-32). Normally, a body was anointed with spices after death (John 19:40). Mary realized that the Lord would soon be taken from them, so she anointed His body for burial while she had the chance. So Mary's act was more than just the common custom of anointing the head of a dinner guest; it was a well-thought-out and reasonable act of worship.

That depth of worship is commended by our Lord and pronounced unforgettable in verse 9. Mary's deed was not a waste of time and effort; it had eternal value. Mary's anointing of Jesus is remembered wherever the gospel message has spread throughout the whole world—it will be remembered forever! The same is true of your worship of God. The worship you direct to God this summer—in whatever job, ministry, or activity He gives you—will never be forgotten.

Let our lips and lives acknowledge God in everything—studies, social life, summer work. Let worship be our way of life.

35

Playing Games With God

1 Samuel 4:3   When the people came into the camp,
the elders of Israel said, "Why has the LORD defeated
us today before the Philistines? Let us take to ourselves from Shiloh the ark of the covenant of the
LORD, that it may come among us and deliver us from
the power of our enemies."
Read all of 1 Samuel 4-7.

There is an interesting book that's been around for
several years, entitled *Games People Play*. It's about the
"games" adults play with each other—mostly selfish and
manipulative—in their interpersonal relationships. It is
to be hoped that growing Christians at least *try* to be
more honest in their relationships, even though we must
confess that we are not immune to such games. However,
playing games with God is an even more serious matter.
Nonbelievers do so habitually. That is unfortunate, but
to be expected. But it is particularly discouraging when
believers are not honest in their relationships with the
Lord.

In 1 Samuel 4-7 we find some examples of people's
playing games with God. At the beginning of chapter 4,
we find that Israel went out to fight their perennial

enemies, the Philistines (4:1). The time was more than one thousand years before Christ, and Israel still did not have a king. For the previous three hundred years or so, it had been ruled by judges—after the time of Joshua, who came after Moses. The people were constantly turning away from the Lord to serve other gods. Thus, God purposely allowed them to be oppressed by their enemies until they cried out in repentance. Then, time and again, the Lord would "pick up the pieces" and send them a deliverer—a judge. Through that judge, God would defeat the enemy, and there would be peace and rest in the land—until the people disobeyed again. By the time of Samuel—sometimes called the last judge and first prophet of Israel, the people of Israel had gone through the cycle at least seven times. No wonder that period is called the dark days of the book of Judges! Again, even during the days of Samuel, that great man of God, Israel was about to go downhill again. How often we growing Christians follow the same pattern!

The Philistines attacked, and Israel was defeated (4:2). Why? We don't read that Israel prayed for guidance and help before the battle. In fact, it seems that Israel had not consulted the Lord through His prophet Samuel for quite some time. They certainly recognized Samuel as a prophet of the Lord (3:20) and knew that he spoke the Word of the Lord (3:21—4:1), but they didn't *obey* the Word. Samuel isn't mentioned again until the beginning of chapter 7. Finally, after more than twenty years, Israel lamented after the Lord (7:2). Only then did the people listen and obey the Word of God spoken by Samuel (7:3-6). Only then did they take advantage of the power of prayer (7:5-9). Only then did the Lord intervene on behalf of Israel (7:10). Only then did Israel defeat the Philistines (7:11-13). And only then was there peace, and Israel progressed (7:14-17).

What a lot of good lessons for us! If we follow the

principles above, we too will have victory in the spiritual battles and struggles for Christian living. God did not record these facts in Scripture just for the historical record! They were "written for our instruction" (Romans 15:4).

When Israel was defeated by the Philistines (1 Samuel 4:2), they began asking, "Why has the Lord defeated us today before the Philistines?" Instead of turning to the Lord for the answer, they decided that, if they merely took the Ark of the Covenant into battle with them, *it* would save them from the Philistines. Notice carefully in verse 3 that the people were not depending on the Lord for help, but on the Ark. They were playing games with God! Let's call it *the game of placating God.* Israel had the superstitious idea that they could manipulate God by use of the Ark.

The Ark was a wooden, boxlike structure overlaid with gold. It symbolically represented the presence and power of God in the midst of His people. To be sure, the Ark played a significant role in the relationship between God and His people (see Exodus 25:10-22). In fact, God promised that His personal presence would be associated with the Ark, if the people would obey and follow Him (Exodus 25:22). But God never confined Himself to a golden box! Perhaps the people remembered the story of how their ancestors had seen the walls of Jericho collapse when they marched around the city with the Ark (Joshua 6). Maybe they thought they could pull off the same kind of victory by its use. But what a difference! The former generation had—by faith—followed direct orders from the Lord (Hebrews 11:30). The new generation was following *form* without *faith.* They had the ritual but no reality. The Ark had become just a talisman to them.

The game of placating God is still played today— religious ritualism without a genuine spiritual relationship with God is certainly placation. Some people "get

religious" around the Christmas holidays and think they
are doing God a favor, in an attempt (maybe unconsciously) to please God by outward actions rather than inward
attitudes. Placating God can be even more subtle, and
growing Christians should be careful. What about wearing crosses and religious medals? Is that an outward
expression of true faith? It can be. But if we think that, by
wearing a religious symbol, we are more protected from
evil or more likely to have our prayers answered, then we
are obviously playing the game. If we think that merely
mouthing the Lord's Prayer or routinely taking communion or carrying a Bible *all* the time will somehow please
God, then we are guilty of playing the game of placating
God. God is neither appeased nor pleased with religious
tokenism.

The Ark by itself was unable to save Israel from the
Philistines (1 Samuel 4). The fact that the wicked priests
Hophni and Phineas (1 Samuel 2) were directly involved
in that futile strategy is a further indication that Israel's
heart was far from the Lord. Not only was Israel soundly
defeated, but the Ark was captured as well. Chapter 5
gives us the record of the Ark of God in Philistine
country. The Philistines played *the game of reducing
God*. They took the Ark and put it in their temple beside
their idol Dagon. As far as they were concerned, that was
a place of honor, and the Israelite god connected with the
Ark deserved to sit beside their own god. After all, this
Hebrew god or gods had the power to bring plagues on
the Egyptians (1 Samuel 4:8). The Philistines did not
deny that there *was* a god for Israel, but they tried to
reduce Him to the level of Dagon, the Philistine fish or
grain god. The Philistines wrongly thought that the Ark
represented a god who would *share* the position of God.

Today, in just about every high school and college in
this country, students are taught that Christianity is just
another religion—one way among many. They are also

taught that the Bible is just one of many good religious
books. Those are obvious examples of unbelievers' trying
to reduce God. Do true Christians ever play the game of
reducing God? Any time our priorities are such that the
Lord is not in first place or is only sharing first place in
our lives, then God is reduced. Our friends and associates
see that our testimony and life-style are inconsistent. God
is apparently reduced even in our minds; otherwise, God
would be *God* in every area of our lives.

Chapter 6 reveals another game that certain Hebrews
played—*the game of disobeying God.* The Philistines
made elaborate plans for returning the Ark to Israel. The
fact that the two milch cows left their calves was proof to
the Philistines that their problems were not merely coin-
cidental (6:9). The God of Israel was supreme—over their
gods, over their health and lives, and over their cattle as
well! At the end of chapter 6, we read that certain men of
Israel were struck down by the Lord, because they dared to
look into the Ark. Why? Because they disobeyed the express written law of God. God had commanded that only
the priests and the Levites were to come near and handle
the Ark. Laymen were not to come near, under penalty of
death (Numbers 1:51). The men who disobeyed were ir-
reverent and took the law of God lightly. They were happy
that the Ark had been returned, but they disobeyed the
Lord. It was not ignorant disobedience, either, because
the Levites were there to inform them.

What a lesson for us! God has given us His Word to
follow and obey. There are many instructions in Scripture
that we might not fully understand or appreciate right
now. For example, the different roles given to men and
women in the family and the church are not always easy
instructions to obey. But to disobey is to play games with
God. And playing games with God is not for growing
Christians.

36

Babies, Beware!

1 John 2:18 Children, it is the last hour; and just as you heard that antichrist is coming, even now many antichrists have arisen; from this we know that it is the last hour.

Read 1 John 2:18-27.

When a healthy new baby is born into the world, there is much joy and excitement within the family. "Isn't that baby just darling?" or "Look at those cute little hands!" are typical exclamations heard during visiting hours on the maternity floor. But it isn't long after the baby arrives home that the hard work and important responsibility of teaching begins. Once the baby begins to crawl and then walk around the house, it is of utmost importance for the young child to receive a course in "beware of dangers." At that stage of growth, it is very important to teach babies not to touch hot stoves or electrical outlets and not to go near basement stairs. The course on how to hold spoons properly can come later!

It is not difficult to see the parallel between the above illustration and the new Christian. When a person is born into the family of God, there is much joy and excitement among the older brothers and sisters—as well as in heaven (see Luke 15:7). But the very important task of teaching begins immediately. And one of the first areas of learning for the new baby in Christ must involve the "bewares." Frequently new Christians get "burned" or hurt, because they were not taught to avoid certain hazardous areas.

In 1 John 2:18-27, new Christians are *directly addressed* and are told to be particularly aware of false teachers and their teaching. The fact that the word "children" is used in verse 18 indicates that recent additions to the family of God are primarily in view. This is not the same word that is translated "children" throughout most of 1 John. In fact, this word for "children" is used only twice in the epistle of 1 John—once in 2:13 and here in 2:18. The word signifies young child or baby, and refers to new believers in the fellowship, in contrast to the "young men" or "fathers" (2:13-14)—those who are more mature or longer in the faith. The more common word that is translated "children" in 1 John signifies the whole family of believers, regardless of growth or number of years in the faith. It refers to all persons who have been born into God's family. That more general term is used in 2:1, 2:12, 2:28, 3:7, 3:18, 4:4, and 5:21. Unfortunately, in our English translations, the distinction between the two words is lost, and it can be very confusing, especially since the more general term is sometimes translated *"little* children." But the phrase "little children" is not used in the sense of lack of *growth,* but rather in the sense of John's *parental affection* for the whole family.

In any case, here in chapter 2, the whole family of believers (v. 12) is broken down into the three different growth categories: fathers, young men, and babies (v. 13). In verses 14-17, the "young men" category of believers is specifically exhorted not to love the world. Certainly that exhortation applies to all Christians, but it is particularly addressed in this context to the "young men." That term by the way, does not mean in contrast to women, but rather the middle growth or maturity level of believers—of *both* sexes. The same holds true for the word "fathers." It is used here for the highest level of growth and maturity. The "fathers" that John was addressing had come to know the Lord as many as *forty years* earlier when the apostle Paul had evangelized the greater Ephesus area.

Well now, that leaves most of us in the "young men" or "baby" categories! And if you are not a brand new Christian, then you are in the "young men" category and are here warned to watch out for the world. "Young men" Christians are particularly vulnerable to the values of this evil world system. Let us remember the three principles of operation of Satan's world system (2:16): appeals to the strong desires of the flesh (pleasure), appeals to the strong desires of the eyes (possessions), and appeals to the pride of life or vanity (power and prestige). Let us not think that our few years as a Christian will make us immune to the attacks of the enemy of our souls. He knows that the "young men" category of believer is very susceptible to the contagious disease of worldliness.

Now let's return to the subject of baby Christians. This category of believers is addressed in verses 18-27, as mentioned above. Because new believers are especially vulnerable to false teaching, this section of Scripture is a loud and clear "beware." You see, new Christians are generally caught up in the joy and excitement of their new life in Christ and are not too preoccupied with worldliness—but they are wide open to the possibility of swallowing false doctrine.

That does not mean that a new Christian is not spiritual. A baby Christian can be just as spiritual as a long-in-the-faith believer. Growth and spirituality are not synonymous terms. It is *growth*, not spirituality, that is in view in the categorizing of believers in this portion of God's Word.

Warning and protection from false teachers are of utmost importance to the proper growth of new Christians. Just as young children must be protected from all the things they try to put into their mouths, so baby Christians must be protected from imbibing false teaching. There are a lot of "wolves in sheep's clothing" around today, just waiting to feed poison to newly-awakened spiritual appetites (see Matthew 7:15). What a responsibility older brothers and sisters have toward the new members of the family! Are you yourself a new Christian? Beware of false teachers and their false doctrine! Not every so-called "spiritual leader" is one of God's gifts to the church!

How can false doctrine be detected? Is there any clue or give-away signal that new Christians should watch for when they come into contact with religious teachers? Yes! Is it their questionable smile? No! Is it their pushiness? No! Is it their pressure to read certain literature? No! Some true servants of God may exhibit all of those "signs."

The sure give-away sign of false teachers is their false *doctrine of Christ*. First John 2:22 tells us that the core of false doctrine is the denial of Jesus Christ as fully God. False teachers may say that Jesus is "divine" or "of God" or "*a* son of God." But they fall short of admitting that *Jesus is God*. Be on the alert for this subtle but very obvious clue! Jehovah's Witnesses, Mormons, Christian Scientists, and Unitarians are just a few of the many cults and sects around today in which one encounters that false teaching. Verse 23 indicates that all who deny the deity of Christ are *not of God!* In fact, they are *antichrists* (vv. 1, 22). They may be very nice and upright and even attending your fellowship, but, as in John's day (v. 19), they are unbelievers—they are not Christians.

Has God given His children any safeguards against the dangers of false doctrine? Yes, of course. Our text inform us that the Scriptures and the Spirit are given to protect us from the dangers of false teaching. Verse 24 refers to the safeguard of Scripture. John's readers were not to let themselves be taken in by the new teachings of the deceivers (v. 26). They were to abide in the Word that they had been taught from the beginning—that is, their conversion (v. 24). The Word of God had been brought to them by the apostles, and they were to let that Word *abide* in them. That is what the new believer needs today for protection from the almost overwhelming waves of false philosophies and insidious teachings that abound in the secular classroom as well as the religious sanctuary. How important it is to take time to teach baby Christians the Word of God!

The Holy Spirit is also a safeguard against false doctrine and is referred to as the "anointing" in verses 20 and 27. Scripture teaches that *all* believers have the Holy Spirit—regardless of growth level! Remember that these verses are particularly addressed to baby Christians, and yet verse 27 clearly indicates that they *all* had the Holy Spirit abiding in them. The statement, "You have no need for anyone to teach you" (v. 27), does not mean that Bible teachers are a waste of time! The point is that new believers need not be sucked in by some *"new* teaching" of the deceivers of verse 26. The Holy Spirit sounds a warning in the believer when the truth is attacked or distorted. The *Word* of God illumined by the *Spirit* of God was, and is, the method by which believers are preserved and protected from false teaching.

37

Case Study in Complaining

Numbers 11:1 Now the people became like those who complain of adversity in the hearing of the Lord; and when the Lord heard it, His anger was kindled, and the fire of the Lord burned among them and consumed some of the outskirts of the camp.

Read all of Numbers 11.

Complaining is so common these days that it could b called a way of life for many people. Just about everybod complains. And why not? There's so much to complai about: teachers, traffic, taxes, and troubles of all kind But they commonness of complaining does not make right. The Word of God comes down pretty hard on th *sin* of complaining. The Bible teaches that complainin is definitely wrong for the growing Christian.

God presents us with a case study in complaining Numbers 11. We not only observe the complaining of th people of Israel; we also gain insight as to the reason behind the complaining. All of this, of course, has application to the growing Christian. In fact, 1 Corin thians 10:11 tells us that what happened in the lives God's people more than three thousand years ago w

200

recorded for us believers in the twentieth century.

The background for Numbers 11 is the journey of Israel through the wilderness. God had brought His people out from the bondage and slavery of Egypt through Moses. They had been to Mount Sinai where the Ten Commandments were given, and now they were moving out toward the land of Canaan—where the country of Israel is today. But they complained all along the way. Because of their murmuring and grumbling, God had to discipline them severely. Some of them actually lost their lives! The Bible is shouting here in Numbers 11 that God does not appreciate complaining. Thus we are exhorted in 1 Corinthians 10:10 not to "grumble, as some of them did, and were destroyed by the destroyer."

We see a couple of different areas of complaining in this eleventh chapter of Numbers. In verse 1 it seems that the people were just complaining about the general *problems* of the trip. There wasn't some single big problem like a famine or an epidemic or a new Pharoah chasing them! No, it was just "normal" complaining about the little nitty-gritty hardships of living and traveling in the wilderness—lugging the tent, same old scenery, another hot day, and so on, and so forth. If it weren't for what the Bible teaches here, we might be inclined to say that theirs was *legitimate* complaining! But the Word of God indicates that "white" griping was uncalled for. The Lord was displeased, and the fire of the Lord consumed some of them.

Do we also complain about the problems of everyday living? What about the food that is set before us at home or in the school dining hall? What about the "unfair" workload that's been dumped on us? What about the irritating things like the weather not meeting our specifications? Yes, those "hardships" may cause us some inconvenience at times, but we are not to complain about them. The Lord always has good reasons for the hardships

He permits to come our way. (Read Deuteronomy 8 to find some reasons for Israel's hardships in the wilderness.)

It is significant that the discipline of the Lord was more active near the outskirts of the camp (v. 1). Most likely it involved the stragglers who were out of order. You see, God had commanded Israel to march and camp in a very precise arrangement (Numbers 2 and 10). Probably those who were on the fringes of the camp were not where they belonged and were voicing their discontent in actions as well as words. It seems that in any Christian fellowship or ministry there are always the "stragglers" or "tagalongs." How often we hear the loudest and sharpest complaints arising from the "fringe group." Are we where we belong in reference to the Lord's people? Or are we possibly on the "outskirts of the camp" where we are "mouthing off"—just asking for the heavy hand of God's discipline? Notice also (v. 2) that God stops the fire of discipline in answer to Moses' prayer. The prayers of God's faithful people for the stragglers of today may have a lot to do with God's high tolerance level of loudmouth complainers!

In verses 4-10 we see that the people of Israel also complained about the *provision* that God had given them. The Lord miraculously provided a daily supply of manna for His people—free bread from heaven! When the manna was first given, the people were very thankful and enjoyed this bread. They said it tasted like wafers with honey (Exodus 16:31). But they began to take the manna for granted and even got sick and tired of it (v. 6). No longer did it have the sweet taste of honey. Now they complained that it had a bland taste of cakes baked with oil (v. 8). Of course the manna itself had not changed— their appreciation of God's provision had changed. But surely Israel should be excused for that kind of complaining! After all, manna flakes for breakfast, manna sandwiches for lunch and manna burgers for supper are not all that appetizing! And yet we read that God was very angry (v. 10). Why? Because the people were not thankful for His gifts. It's true that the manna was not caviar or lobster, but it was good and nourishing food for the demanding journey. Rather than thanking the Lord for His daily provision, the people complained and longed for the more spicy foods of Egypt (v. 5).

Are we content with what God has provided for us? There are many practical ways in which this story could be applied, but let's think for a minute of the spiritual provision that God has made for us in Christ. In John 6, the Lord Jesus spoke of the manna, and then went on to show that He is the true Bread out of heaven. As the manna was God's means of maintaining the physical life of His people, so Christ is the way in which the believer's spiritual life is sustained. Growing Christians must feed on Christ. He is not only the source of our spiritual life; He is the sustenance for that life. (Read all of John 6.)

Are we satisfied with Christ? Or are we complaining about being "unfulfilled"? God's Word teaches that all we need for complete and total fulfillment is found in our Lord Jesus Christ. But the problem with many of us is that we still desire "the leeks and the garlic" of our former lives (Numbers 11:5). The people of Israel complained of being unfulfilled because they began to long for the things of Egypt from which they had been delivered. The Christian who still craves the things of this world will be unfulfilled spiritually. If our "tastebuds" are excited by strong desires to experience what this world has to offer, or to accumulate the material things of this world, or to get ahead in this world, then the things of Christ will taste flat and bland. Where are your tastebuds?

The Lord's reaction to Israel's complaints about His provision teaches another important lesson. In verses 18-20, God informed Moses that He would give the people meat to eat. He would give them exactly what they craved and in such abundance that it would "come out of their noses" and be "loathsome" to them! Sure enough, that's exactly what happened, and in greedy hoarding of the meat they experienced God's heavy hand of discipline once again (vv. 31-35). The Christian whose soul whines for the things of this world may get his wish. But God will grant the request in such a way that His fatherly discipline will be included. What kind of Father would God be if our unchecked cravings did not bring serious consequences? Let us not think that, just because God has allowed us to have our hearts' desires, we have His approval! This lesson is encapsulated for us in the experience of the Israelites, as they ". . . craved intensely in the wilderness, and tempted God in the desert. So He gave them their request, but sent a wasting disease among them" (Psalm 106:14-15).

The sin of complaining was one reason why Israel wandered in the wilderness for forty long years. It took only a few hours to get the people out of Egypt, but it took forty years to get Egypt out of the people. Is it possible that we are "wandering in the wilderness" of Christian living because of the sin of complaining? We may have it all together in the areas of doctrine and commitment, but we go on griping just the same. Complaining, of course, is just the surface symptom of a much deeper problem—discontent. That is why the Bible so strongly condemns complaining. The murmurings and grumblings of complaint are evidence that we are dissatisfied with the way God is leading our lives. The solution to the problem is to recognize our sin and then realize and acknowledge that our heavenly Father always knows what's best for us—even down to the little problems He allows us to face. Let us stop our complaining so that our own lives do not become case studies in complaining.

38

Abortion is Appalling

Psalm 51:5 Behold, I was brought forth in iniquity, and in sin my mother conceived me.

Exodus 21:22-24 And if men struggle with each other and strike a woman with child so that she has a miscarriage, yet there is no further injury, he shall surely be fined as the woman's husband may demand of him; and he shall pay as the judges decide. But if there is any further injury, then you shall appoint as a penalty life for life, eye for eye, tooth for tooth, hand for hand, foot for foot.

Webster defines the word *appalling* as "inspiring horror, dismay, or disgust." This word is certainly an appropriate adjective to describe the abortion situation today. Abortion is appalling, not only because of the current statistics, but also because of the unchanging standards of Scripture.

Statistics obviously cannot tell the whole story, but they certainly do point up the alarming evidence that the story of abortion is truly appalling. Since the watershed decision of the Supreme Court in 1973, which declared that the unborn fetus is not a legal person under the

Constitution of the United States, as many as 7 million
surgical abortions have been performed in this country.
The present rate of abortions in the United States is about
1.5 million per year, and the rate continues to increase.
We reacted with horror and anger when the lives of 6
million innocent Jews were taken during the Holocaust.
Is it not equally appalling that 7 million babies have
been intentionally destroyed? The total number of American war casualties throughout our country's history—
including *all* wars from the War for Independence to Viet
Nam—is only a fraction (less than 1/5) of the number of
unborn babies that have been killed by legalized abortion.
In fact, there are now more unborn babies killed by
surgical abortion each year in the United States than the
total number of American war casualties.

The decision of the Supreme Court to permit Congress
to limit federal funding for certain abortions is a tiny step
in the right direction, but falls far short of changing the
appalling trend. Over four thousand unborn babies continue to be killed each day in the United States—some by
the suction method, which tears and mutilates the tiny
body; some by the "D and C" technique, which slices and
scrapes until the womb is clean; some by saline poisoning,
which burns the tender skin of the unborn; and some by
abdominal surgery, if the fetus is too large for other
methods. In some "Caesarian section" abortions, the baby
fights for its life and, if wanted, could be kept alive. But
those unwanted babies are left to die! Not one of those
four thousand innocent babies is protected by law in the
decision concerning his or her destruction. How tragic!
How sad!

Does the Bible have anything to say about abortion?
When we consult a biblical concordance, we find that the
word "abortion" is not listed. However, the Scriptures
deal very definitely with the most basic question involved
in the abortion issue. Is the fetus a human individual?

Psalm 51 is David's great prayer of repentance after his sin with Bathsheba. In verse 5, David acknowledges that "in sin my mother conceived me." That does not mean that David was an illegitimate child or that sex is sinful. What David is saying is that he had a sinful nature from *conception*. The *New International Version* is a helpful translation at this point: "Surely I have been a sinner from birth, sinful from the time my mother conceived me." That is not just David's poetic way of reflecting on his beginning. It is the Word of God, teaching us that we have a sinful nature from the time of our conception. We don't become sinners when we commit our first sin. We are not just born with a sinful nature—we are *conceived* with it.

In light of this teaching of Scripture, let us ask ourselves a couple of vitally important questions in reference to the abortion issue. Does a "blob of protoplasm" have a sinful nature? If the unborn fetus is merely a "piece of tissue," would the Bible attribute a sinful nature to it? The scriptural evidence from both Old and New Testaments is that the sinful nature is uniquely and inseparably associated with human life that begins at conception.

A number of other Scriptures support the basic truth that the fetus is a person. Consider Psalm 139:13-16 and Jeremiah 1:4-5 for example. Both David and Jeremiah speak of themselves as persons *before* birth. In Luke 1:44, we read that John the Baptist leaped in his mother's womb for joy. A "blob of protoplasm" can hardly experience the emotion of joy. Joy is a human emotion. Some will argue that that was only Elizabeth's way of speaking about the unborn baby's kicking in her womb. But let's be careful about handling Scripture this way. It is true that historical contexts and cultural settings must be taken into account when interpreting Scripture, but always remember that the Holy Spirit is the ultimate Author of Scripture, and His inspiration extends to its very words (see 1 Corinthians 2:13). Is it not possible that God is teaching us something about the human fetus in Luke 1:44?

The doctrine of the incarnation is that the eternal Son of God became man—*human*. When did the incarnation take place? At Jesus' birth? At the point of viability? At the moment of quickening? Or was it at conception? Matthew 1:20 "nudges" us toward the conclusion that the incarnation took place at conception. The angel comforted Joseph concerning Mary by telling him that "that which has been conceived in her is of the Holy Spirit."

In view of those Scriptures, is it possible to come to any logical conclusion other than that the fetus is a person? A Supreme Court ruling about when personhood begins in no way changes the infallible and eternal Word of God. Unborn babies are human individuals from the moment of conception, as far as God is concerned. Dare we take a position that condones abortion or is even neutral concerning this issue?

Any discussion of what the Bible says about abortion would not be complete without an explanation of Exodus 21:22-24. Some pro-abortionists have ripped this passage out of its context and said that it gives a biblical basis for abortion. These verses *in no way* support abortion. In fact, if a premature birth or miscarriage occurred, then the guilty one was fined—punished. If the mother died as well, the guilty one would pay with his life. We are certainly not to conclude from this that the dead fetus was considered less than human. All that this passage is saying in this seemingly more lenient view is that an offender was not to be considered a murderer for causing an *accidental miscarriage.* Those who try to justify *intentional surgical abortion* on the basis of this Scripture grossly misinterpret and misapply the Bible.

The sanctity of human life is undeniably supported throughout the entire Bible. Our responsibility before

God is to protect human life—born and unborn. To intentionally terminate the life of an unborn baby is wrong—regardless of circumstances, culture, or courts.

Countless people today, often well-meaning individuals, are confused and brainwashed concerning abortion. As Christians, we should take every opportunity to speak out against abortion. But growing Christians should not only *speak*. We should reach out in compassion to those who are desperately struggling to do the right thing in regard to the appalling issue of abortion.

39

Expect to be Persecuted

1 Peter 4:12 Beloved, do not be surprised at the fiery
ordeal among you, which comes upon you for your
testing, as though some strange thing were happening to you.

Read 1 Peter 4:12-19.

The Bible never commands or exhorts Christians to
pray for persecution. But the Bible very definitely tells the
growing Christian to *expect* persecution. 1 Peter 4:12
emphatically states that we are not to be surprised when
persecution comes, or think that "some strange thing" is
happening to us when we are persecuted as Christians
(see also Acts 14:22; Philippians 1:29; 2 Timothy 3:12; 1
John 3:13). Persecution is "part of the package" of our
salvation!

By no means is such a statement meant to imply that
the salvation of our souls is earned or merited through
suffering a certain amount of persecution. No, clearly the
Bible teaches that salvation is a personal gift from God,
and persecution is not part of the price. The price of our
salvation was fully paid by God Himself when our Lord
Jesus suffered and died on the cross for our sins. But
although persecution is not part of the purchasing price

of our salvation, it certainly *is* part of the "path of progress" of our salvation. We do not "get saved" by suffering persecution, but when we are saved we will suffer persecution. Such a concept as "saved to suffer" may rattle us a little at first. It may even cause us to think a few wrong thoughts about our God. But such negative vibrations are cancelled out when we see from Scripture that God has a number of purposes for permitting His children to be persecuted.

In the book of 1 Peter, God tells us a lot about persecution. In fact, this book of the Bible could be called a handbook on suffering persecution. It was written just before the outbreak of the Roman persecutions under Nero in A.D. 64. First Peter 4:12 could be looked on as a prophecy of the coming Roman persecutions of the Christian church. But of course, 1 Peter 4:12 is applicable to Christians of all time. Christians of the twentieth century should expect to be persecuted for their faith as the Christians of the first century were.

It should be stressed at this point that wherever the book of 1 Peter talks about suffering, it is not just any kind of suffering. Christians suffer heart attacks and car accidents and depleted bank accounts and missed appointments and bad colds, but those are not the kinds of suffering that Peter has in mind. Those are problems, to be sure, and God can use all of them in our Christian lives for our ultimate benefit (see Romans 8:28-29). However, the sufferings of 1 Peter are persecutions that come upon the Christian precisely because he is a Christian—slander, reproach, mockery, scorn, put-downs, cut-downs, verbal abuse, social ostracism, physical torture, and even martyrdom.

Have you experienced any nonphysical persecution and hate on your campus or on your job because you're a Christian? Maybe you've suffered a lower grade in a course or even lost a job or promotion because of your

Christian testimony. That is all part of normal Christian living and should be *expected*. In some countries, even physical persecution is a way of life for Christians.

Several of God's reasons for permitting His children to suffer persecution are given in the verses immediately following 1 Peter 4:12. First of all there is the *reward of blessing*. Verse 13 speaks about the blessing of future glory, and verse 14 refers to the blessing of present glory. If we are willing to share in the sufferings of Christ *now*, we will share in His glory when He returns. Romans 8:17 says that "we suffer with Him in order that we may also be glorified with Him." The Lord Jesus said, in reference to persecution for His sake, "Rejoice, and be glad, for your reward in heaven is great" (Matthew 5:10-12).

The Bible does not tell us all the specifics of what's involved in our sharing of Christ's glory. However, we do know that when the effects of sin are completely erased from this universe, the untainted glory of God will be manifested throughout His creation forever. This glory will be focused and centered in the person of Christ and His redeeming work (see Philippians 2:5-11). We have the opportunity now of investing in that future glory. Just think: today we have the privilege of participating in, and contributing to, the future honor and praise and splendor of our Savior—if we are willing to suffer a little persecution. Such a high and holy calling should help us to endure the "Holy Joe" and "religious nut" scorn that we often experience—or *should* experience!

It should be emphasized that our sharing the sufferings of Christ as mentioned in 1 Peter 4:13 has nothing to do with Christ's sufferings on the cross. Those sufferings paid for our sins and were completed when Christ proclaimed triumphantly from the cross, "It is finished" (John 19:30). The sufferings of Christ in which we share now are sufferings for the sake of Christ—namely persecution. They are called the sufferings of Christ, because

the church—the Body of Christ on earth—suffers whenever Christians are persecuted for the name of Christ
(Colossians 1:24). Remember that the resurrected Christ
questioned Saul on the Damascus road, saying "Why do
you persecute Me?" as Saul was on his way to persecute
Christians (Acts 9:4). But the church persecuted now will
be the church glorified soon, when Christ's Body on earth
is united with her Head in heaven.

There is also a present glory associated with being
persecuted for Christ. First Peter 4:14 informs us that the
Holy Spirit of Glory rests upon us when we are reviled
for the name of Christ. All believers have the Holy Spirit
dwelling in them (Romans 8:9-11; 1 Corinthians 12:13;
Ephesians 1:13), but persecuted believers have the Holy
Spirit *resting* on them. The persecuted Christian comes
to know more of the reality of the presence of God in his
life. The relationship becomes deeper and more intimate—
much more than is possible if the believer is unwilling to
suffer. The relationship that develops between two soldiers going through the thick of battle together is much
closer than a peacetime friendship. Remember, it's only
on earth that we have the privilege of enlarging our
relationship with our Lord in *this* way. There is no
persecution in heaven!

After stressing (1 Peter 4:15-16) that suffering for the
sake of Christ has nothing whatsoever to do with suffering for our own wrongdoing, Peter moves on to mention
another reason why God allows persecution. In verses
17-19 the emphasis is on the *renewal of commitment* that
results from the suffering of persecution. In verse 17 the
emphasis is on collective commitment. Judgment of "the
household of God" (v. 17) is not discipline in the punitive
sense, but rather discipline in the preventive sense. The
persecution of the church, God's household, is a safeguard
against worldliness and waywardness. Persecution has a
purifying effect on the church. Tertullian, a second-cen-

tury Christian, said that "the blood of martyrs is the seed
of the church." Throughout her history, the church has
not only survived during times of persecution, but she
has been purified. If the church in America today were to
undergo extreme physical persecution, we would see quite
a few nominal Christians and other hangers-on "leave
the ship." Persecution makes us "tested by fire" to prove
our faith (1 Peter 1:7).

Widespread and prolonged persecution will produce
renewal of commitment of the church as a whole, and
any persecution endured by the individual Christian will
generally result in greater personal commitment to the
Lord. Christians will not only have "ceased from sin" to
lead more holy lives (1 Peter 4:1-4), but they will "entrust
their souls to a faithful Creator in doing what is right"
(v. 19). What words could better describe what Christian
renewal is all about? Social ostracism and slander and
scorn from fellow students and fellow employees will not
turn off the *growing* Christian; it will drive the believer
closer to the Lord Jesus.

Although persecution of the believer is to be expected
and is "according to the will of God" (v. 19), let us
remember that it is a family matter. We are the "beloved"
(v. 12) children of the "faithful Creator" (v. 19) who
always has our best interests in view. Verses 17 and 18
remind us of the vast difference between the persecution
of the believer in this life and the punishment of the
godless unbeliever who refused to obey the gospel of
God in the next life. The Christian who understands
God's reasons for allowing persecution not only expects
to be persecuted but is willing to suffer it.

40

Turning the Other Cheek

Matthew 5:38-42 "You have heard that it was said,
'AN EYE FOR AN EYE, AND A TOOTH FOR A TOOTH.' But
I say to you, do not resist him who is evil; but
whoever slaps you on your right cheek, turn to him
the other also. And if anyone wants to sue you, and
take your shirt, let him have your coat also. And
whoever shall force you to go one mile, go with him
two. Give to him who asks of you, and do not turn
away from him who wants to borrow from you."
Read Matthew 5-7.

The Sermon on the Mount (Matthew 5-7) has always
been considered one of the most beautiful and moving
portions of Scripture. Well, no wonder! The words were
spoken by our Lord Himself. What a tremendous effect
the church would have on this unbelieving world if we
growing Christians practiced more of the principles given
to us in that wonderful sermon.

But how do we practice those principles? There are
some "impossible" commandments in this part of the
Word of God. Look, for example, at Matthew 5:38-42.
Does this mean that I am to "turn the other cheek" any
time someone punches me in the face? Can't I defend

myself and "resist him who is evil"? Can't I at least run
away and not expose my "other cheek"? And what about
the matter of the shirt and coat in verse 40? You mean to
say that, if someone rips off my car radio, I should give
him my car as well? You've got to be kidding! As to going
two miles instead of one (v. 41), I've got to disobey here.
People are always twisting my arm and manipulating
me. If I didn't draw the line somewhere, I wouldn't even
have time to read my Bible and pray! And certainly the
Lord doesn't expect me to give to everyone who comes
along with a handout (v. 42). Why, there are so many "con
men" and "beggars" in my dorm that I'd be wiped out
overnight if I put that principle into practice!

Does the above reasoning sound like your own thought
patterns when you're confronted with such demanding
directions from our Lord? It's only natural to think that
way. But is that the way we are to take those difficult statements in the Sermon on the Mount? What is the correct
interpretation of the Scripture, and what is the proper
application of it today?

One of the primary rules of biblical interpretation is
that you never try to figure out what a particular passage
means without taking into account the surrounding Scripture. That is, you don't pull a Scripture out of context.
The context of Matthew 5:38-42 is a discourse by Christ
(Matthew 5:17-48) within the Sermon on the Mount on
the Old Testament law of Moses. The most pressing
questions in the minds of those who heard the new
teachings of our Lord would obviously concern the Old
Testament laws, which were their way of life. Was Jesus
setting aside the law of Moses? Was He advocating a
radical departure from the mind of God revealed in the
Old Testament Scriptures?

God's standards of righteousness do not change, nor do
His plans, as revealed in the Scriptures. Jesus said, "I did
not come to abolish, but to fulfill" (v. 17). Christ had

actually come to fulfill, or make complete, the whole scope of the Law and the Prophets. He alone could explain and reveal the true and full meaning of the Scriptures. Therefore, *His* interpretation and teaching of the law of Moses would be the correct view—not the teachings of the scribes and Pharisees, who were self-proclaimed teachers of the law. Christ's understanding of the requirements of the law of Moses would be the interpretation God had originally intended.

The fact that the scribes and Pharisees misunderstood the requirements and intentions of the law underlies our Lord's statement in verse 20. Their view was far below the divine view. Over the years the Mosaic legislation had been so twisted and distorted, misinterpreted and misapplied, "watered down" and "added to" that the scribes and Pharisees of Christ's day were way off target in their ideas of following the law (Matthew 15:1-3). They were so far off that they gave equal authority to their traditions, and some of them actually thought that they were keeping the righteous requirements of the law by their outward show of religiosity. In order to correct those wrong views, the Lord Jesus selected six areas of the law of Moses, which had been misinterpreted through the oral tradition of the scribes and Pharisees. Those areas are covered in verses 21-48. Murder, adultery, divorce, vows, retaliation, and enmity all needed reinterpretation, because of the gross misunderstandings of the Pharisees.

It is significant that the Lord Jesus did not begin His comments on each of the six areas with the words, "It is written . . ." but rather with the words, "You have heard that it was said . . ." (vv. 21, 27, 31, 33, 38, 43). In other words, He was not just commenting on the particular Scriptures He had in mind, but the wrong ideas that had been built up around them as well. For example, He said (v. 43), "You have heard that it was said, 'YOU SHALL LOVE YOUR NEIGHBOR, and hate your enemy.'" To "love your neighbor" was certainly part of the Mosaic legislation (Leviticus 19:18), but to "hate your enemy" was not. That was part of the faulty oral tradition of the scribes and Pharisees. The Lord went on (v. 44) to correct that misunderstanding, telling them to love their enemies and to pray for those who persecuted them. The Lord Jesus was not changing the law, nor was He adding something new to it; rather, He was interpreting the law's requirements, as God had originally given them.

In verses 38-42, the Lord dealt with what has become known as the *lex talionis* (law of retaliation). The scribes and Pharisees had taken this area of the law and twisted it to justify selfish acts of personal vengeance. "AN EYE FOR AN EYE, AND A TOOTH FOR A TOOTH" (v. 38) was never given by God for personal revenge and retaliation. Each time that law is mentioned in the Old Testament (Exodus 21:24; Leviticus 24:20; Deuteronomy 19:21), the context is civil justice—not individual "tit-for-tat." God gave the law as a civil restrictive measure and not as a personal permissive liberty. "Let the punishment fit the crime" was God's direction for law and order. The court could not gouge out the eye of a defendant who had merely given someone a black eye! The public magistrate could not pull every tooth of a man who had merely punched someone in the mouth!

The Lord came down hard on the scribes and Pharisees at this point. He explained that, in the areas of personal relationships, we are to "turn the other cheek" and "go the extra mile." How far are we to carry this principle today? Certainly we are not to carry on personal vendettas. God promises us that He will take care of those problems in His own way (Romans 12:19).

But what if a thief breaks into my house, beats up my family, and cleans out the place completely? Should I "turn the other cheek" and not try to defend myself and my family? Should I "go the extra mile" and show him

the $100 hidden on the top closet shelf and then help him
to load up his truck with my furniture? No, of course not!
Remember that the context of this Scripture concerns
personal revenge and retaliation, not the matter of defense
in an assault or attack, and not the matter of justice
where civil laws are broken.

If a thief must be brought to justice before the state, the
state, under God, is still to operate on the principle of
"AN EYE FOR AN EYE, AND A TOOTH FOR A TOOTH." Our
Lord in no way changed that principle of civil law. You
can imagine the crime and chaos that would result if our
civil courts operated on the principle of "turning the
other cheek." Remember that we are citizens of state, as
well as citizens of heaven. We have a responsibility to see
that civil justice is carried out. We would be irresponsible
before the state—as well as encouraging evil—if we were
to just forget about the crime.

What about the person who knocks at my door and
asks for a contribution for himself or for some agency
that is undeserving or unscriptural? The Lord does not
ask us to give indiscriminately of our time and money to
every freeloader who comes along (see 2 Thessalonians
3:10-12). He is, however, opposing the selfish and miserly
spirit of the scribes and Pharisees. Confronted with persons in real need, they gave grudgingly and reluctantly, if
they gave at all. That type of giving should not characterize the growing Christian. We are to help all who ask, as
long as their requests do not contradict Scripture.

Interpreted properly, the "impossible" commands of
Matthew 5:38-42 are indeed possible—possible, but not
easy. Many times the obedient Christian will be "stepped
on," yet we are called to endure and not to retaliate. When
someone insults or excludes us, takes advantage of us, or
talks behind our backs, we are to "turn the other cheek"
and not to seek revenge. It may hurt us (v. 39), cost us (v.
40), inconvenience us (v. 41), or exhaust us (v. 42). There

will always be those borderline cases, in which we must make decisions—sometimes very painful ones. Yet, even in those situations, remember that mercy has always been God's "rule of thumb."